The Author Event Primer

The Author Event Primer

How to Plan, Execute and Enjoy
Author Events

Chapple Langemack

LIBRARIES
UNLIMITED
A Member of the Greenwood Publishing Group

Westport, Connecticut • London

Library of Congress Cataloging-in-Publication Data

Langemack, Chapple.
  The author event primer : how to plan, execute and enjoy author events /
  by Chapple Langemack.
      p. cm.
  Includes bibliographical references and index.
  ISBN-13: 978-1-59158-302-8 (alk. paper)
  ISBN-10: 1-59158-302-0 (alk. paper)
  1. Public libraries—Cultural programs—United States—Handbooks,
  manuals, etc. 2. Libraries—Cultural programs—Handbooks, manuals, etc.
  3. Libraries and community—Handbooks, manuals, etc. 4. Reading
  promotion—Handbooks, manuals, etc. 5. Libraries—Marketing—Handbooks,
  manuals, etc. 6. Authors and readers. I. Title.
  Z716.4.L36   2007
  021.2'6—dc22   2006032405

British Library Cataloguing in Publication Data is available.

Library of Congress Catalog Card Number: 2006032405
ISBN-13: 978-1-59158-302-8
ISBN-10: 1-59158-302-0

First published in 2007

Libraries Unlimited, 88 Post Road West, Westport, CT 06881
A Member of the Greenwood Publishing Group, Inc.
www.lu.com

Printed in the United States of America

The paper used in this book complies with the
Permanent Paper Standard issued by the National
Information Standards Organization (Z39.48–1984).

10 9 8 7 6 5 4 3 2 1

*For Debbie, frequent partner in crime,
and for Virginia and Marcia, two cool tomatoes*

Contents

Acknowledgments

I am both indebted and honored by the generosity of spirit and willingness to share best practices I encountered while gathering information for this book. Librarians, authors, agents, publishing folk, media escorts, development officers, booksellers, and publicists all took time they didn't really have to respond to my questions and make me aware of issues I hadn't previously considered. I thank you all.

Steven Barclay
Judy Butler
Barbara Carmody
Sue Cozzens
Cuyahoga County Public Library
	Foundation, Ohio
Dakota County Library, Minnesota
Davis County Library, Utah
Des Moines Public Library, Iowa
Deirdre Devlin
Darlene Dineen
David Domkoski
Laura Dudnik
Evanston Public Library, Illinois
Sari Feldman
Lisa Fernow
Lisa Fraser
Jane Graham George
Pete Giacoma
Susan Gibney
Michael Harkovitch
HarperCollins Publishers
Chris Higashi
Lisa Hill
Jan Kaiser
King County Library System,
	Washington
Holly Koelling

Martin County Library, Florida
Nancy McGill
New York Public Library, New York
Christopher Orth
Sandra Payne
Dick Pahle
Darlene Pearsall
Sally Porter
Public Library of Charlotte and
	Mecklenburg County, North
	Carolina
Marcia Lane Purcell
Random House Publishers
Kim Ricketts
Sharyn Rosenblum
Rita Rouse
Salt Lake County Library System,
	Utah
Deborah Schneider
Judi Snyder
Virginia Stanley
Tacoma Public Library, Washington
Toledo-Lucas County Public
	Library, Ohio
Washington Center for the Book,
	Seattle
Westlake Porter Public Library, Ohio
Claire Wilkinson
Constance Younkin

1

Why Author Visits?

For readers, authors are magical beings. They take us places we never thought we'd see and show us things we never imagined. They can engage our emotions for people and circumstances far outside our own experience, or they can reflect precisely what's written in our own hearts. They are wondrous beings, these authors, and once they've engaged us so skillfully on the page, we're often left wondering what they themselves are like. We're curious as to how and why their work came to be. Sometimes we feel a kinship so strong that sitting down with our favorite author over a beer or a cup of coffee seems like the most natural thing in the world. While an iced tea with Rick Bragg and a chat about *All Over but the Shoutin'* might not be in the offing for most of us, an author event certainly can be. Oh, I know at least one person who claims not to want to meet an author in the flesh. She says it would destroy the mystery, that she doesn't want to be disillusioned. The funny thing is, I often see her at author events.

The potential benefits of author events are many and varied. Author programming may well help your agency

- promote books and reading.
- establish the library's role as the "life of the mind" for the greater community.
- enrich and expand your patrons' (or customer's) reading experience.
- create a buzz in your community with newsworthy names.

- provide a hook for bringing people into your venue.
- reach out to portions of the community who may not have discovered your library or organization.
- create a sense of community by giving the public a focus and reason to gather.
- raise funds.
- build connections with other community organizations.

Now let's explore some of these great outcomes in a little more detail.

Fulfilling the Library's Mission

For libraries, author programming is a natural outgrowth of their mission of connecting readers and writers. Intellectual stimulation, generating excitement about books and reading, that's all right down the library's alley as far as I'm concerned. And when you're able to bring the community along on that mission, here's the kind of feedback you get:

The Charlotte Observer

Saturday, October 24, 1998

Bravo, Novello

Thousands turn out for library's Festival of Reading

… The library is extremely important to Mecklenburg's life and Mecklenburg's success. Support for Novello is a reminder to elected officials, educators and others that this community is serious about seeing that adults can explore the life of the mind and about preparing children to enjoy it.

Expanding the Story

By offering author programming, you are, in effect, expanding the story for your readers. As enjoyable as a Ridley Pearson thriller might be on its own, it's even better when you hear the charming Mr. Pearson talk about the genesis for the idea in person. You have now added dimensions to your reading experience

The Washington Center for the Book (WCB) at the Seattle Public Library put author visits on the map with their Seattle Reads program. I asked Chris Higashi, Associate Executive Director for WCB, what she and former Executive Director Nancy Pearl had in mind when they came up with the idea for an entire city reading the same book. Here's what she told me:

"We created If All of Seattle Read the Same Book with the belief that a reader's appreciation of and engagement in a work of literature is broadened and deepened through hearing other readers' responses to the same book. Why? Because everyone reads a different book, because we each bring our own background, culture, life experiences to the reading of a book."

So, in Chris's view, there's yet another layer. Not only is your reading experience enriched by hearing the author talk about his work, you can gain insight by hearing the opinions—and questions—of other audience members. As Chris says, even though we're each reading the same book, we each internalize a different story, depending on our own experiences. And sharing our responses with the nexus of an author visit can be particularly satisfying.

Author visits also serve a readers' advisory function. You are connecting readers and writers, exposing your patrons to books and authors unfamiliar to them. You are offering an opportunity for discovery. Here's a note one of our patrons wrote after attending an author series:

> I wish to express my pleasure and gratitude for the Author! Author! series. The program was very well run and the authors entertaining. I particularly enjoyed Mark Salzman and Malachy McCourt. Listening to the authors has encouraged me to read a wider selection of their respective works.
>
> I hope this program will be continued in the future. I look forward to the next selection of authors....

Expanding stories and readers' horizons are great benefits to author visits, but there are other pluses as well.

Creating a Buzz

Mention libraries to a reporter, and you'll likely get a big yawn. The occasional censorship flap notwithstanding, libraries just aren't perceived as exciting places. (Wait 'til they see my script for the library reality series!) However, an author event can generate some buzz and get visibility in the media that you might not otherwise get. I used to think that any kind of programming was worth doing solely because it let the community know that there was something exciting going on at the library—even if they didn't show up for the program. I've amended that view somewhat over the years, but I still believe that an exciting event, particularly an author event, is a good way to create some excitement in the press and in the community.

Inspired by a program at the Public Library Association Conference, the Board of Directors of the Davis County Library in Utah decided several years ago that the library should begin author programming. Pete Giacoma, the Library Director, recounts that he didn't think it was such a great idea: "I had never been convinced that adult programming could succeed relative to the amount of effort that has to be invested in a quality event; but the Board was intent, and I started the work."

Pete assigned staff member Judy Butler to the task. Judy began by hosting Orson Scott Card, hoping that 100 people might come. In fact, 700 people came. Judy cycled 250 people at a time through the auditorium, and Mr. Card repeated his program for each new audience. From there the author event program grew and grew. To date Davis County Library has hosted such notables as Anne Perry, Ivan Doig, Michael Deaver, Richard Paul Evans, Andrea Mitchell and Teri Garr.

Pete is now a believer in buzz: "These programs have allowed us to expand and enhance the role we play in the community in a manner that appears greatly appreciated by those who attend them but also by the broader public who see high-visibility individuals visiting our community. Traditionally, such individuals visit Salt Lake City; that they now visit Davis County—and I hope I am not overstating the point here—gives the community a sense of having arrived, of some stature as a place, of a literary interest that complements other cultural organizations—the art center, the community theater—in the area. For us, for the library staff, our ability to offer programs that attract attendees from fifty, a hundred and, on occasion, hundred of miles away, literally leads us to imagine that we have helped elevate our visibility as a public agency committed to quality service."

Reaching Out

If you don't think you can bring people into the library, how about taking the event to them? Our library system often works with schools to bring authors in for a visit. It gives the author a guaranteed audience, and it gives us the chance to promote the library to kids who might not otherwise go. I guarantee that bringing in someone like *Holes* author Louis Sachar or Laurie Halse Anderson, the National Book Award finalist for *Speak,* for a school visit will make you and your library a hero to both students and staff.

Reaching Out: Taking Authors to Schools

King County Library System (KCLS) has been bringing authors to students for several years with gratifying results. Deborah Schneider, Programming Coordinator for KCLS, has this to say about bringing authors into schools:

Our librarians tell me that students respond to author visits in the schools by showing up at the library. They feel a connection with the staff member who introduces the author and often does a short booktalk. Students come in search of the books and to remind the librarian that they've "met" before.

My personal experience in escorting authors to the schools for KCLS has also shown me the impact of such programming. I remember taking poet Mel Glenn (author of Class Dismissed! and many other books of poetry) to one of the schools in the county with a hugely diverse population. They had suffered losing a student in a drive-by shooting the previous week. Mel not only captured the attention of these kids, he had them begging the school librarian for his books. We were stopped in the hallway by a student who recited his own poetry to Mel. Kids talked about Mel's visit for days afterward. It was a warm, fuzzy experience for everyone, including Mel, who left his e-mail address so that kids could stay in touch with him.

The poet Kurtis Lamkin evoked a similar response in students. Kurtis often accompanies his poetry with the Kora, an African musical instrument. One of our stops was an alternative high school in a small town in the foothills of the Cascade Mountains. They were a noisy and appreciative audience, and following his performance, they had a break. As we walked to the car to load Kurtis's Kora, one of the students started singing, "My body, my body, my bod-ey," one of Kurtis's poems. Soon others joined in to serenade us out of the parking lot.

I think taking these programs to schools is one of the most effective means to educate students about the services we offer and to invite them into our libraries.

Creating Community

The All City Reading concept was a masterstroke because it did so many things so well. It created lots of opportunities for readers to enhance their experience with a particular book by hearing what the author and each other had to say. It certainly created a buzz—not only in Seattle but also around the country. And it created community as well. Here's Chris Higashi's take on it:

> The longer we do the project, the more I see how we create community, bonds amongst our patrons and members of the public, through the shared experience of people—across ages, generations, cultures, ethnic backgrounds, economic levels—reading and discussing a work of literature.
>
> Julie Otsuka spent four days in Seattle and made seven appearances to talk with readers about *When the Emperor Was Divine*. She connected beautifully with audiences, was warm, generous, articulate and funny. Ms. Otsuka had toured twice for her novel, but "Seattle Reads" was a whole other experience—to meet and talk with so many former internees.
>
> Many older Nisei (second-generation Japanese Americans) came to each of the events. The majority were people attending their first Seattle Public Library program. One memorable moment occurred the first evening, at our Beacon Hill Branch near the International District in Seattle. We noticed a number of Japanese Americans in the audience and asked former internees to please stand. From all parts of the room, thirty people rose. The crowd murmured, "Oh ..." and applauded. It was so moving; we all cried. It was probably the first time these people had had their internment acknowledged by the community.
>
> Though it was not our intent, I believe what happened was that in featuring this novel, we honored people in our own community who lived through the experience. It's one thing to read about the internment, and it's quite another to come face to face with people who lived through it. Many have described this year's Seattle Reads as the finest since we invented it.

The community came together in an unexpected way when Orson Scott Card made his visit to Davis County, Utah, for its inaugural author event that I mentioned earlier in the chapter. Judy, the program organizer, was tickled to notice that punked-out teens with Mohawk hairdos were sitting companionably next to more conservative church ladies, representing fans of both Mr. Card's science fiction works like *Ender's Game* (which won both the Hugo and Nebula Awards) and his historical fiction based on Bible stories. Building community was always part of the plan for Davis County author events, and the result was gratifying. Library Director Pete Giacoma says, "We offer refreshments and sweets after the presentation to encourage people to sit and talk with each other and with us."

Raising Funds

Another Side

"See Another Side of the Eastside," the second annual luncheon to benefit the East King County office of Habitat for Humanity, is scheduled for noon Wednesday at the DoubleTree Hotel in Bellevue.

Pulitzer Prize–winning author David K. Shipler, author of *The Working Poor: Invisible in America,* is the keynote speaker. Dennis Bounds of KING 5 TV is the emcee.

Last year's event luncheon raised nearly $200,000 for the cause. For information or to reserve a seat, contact Mary Martin at 425.869.6007 or mary@habitatekc.org.

Author events can also serve as fundraisers. Although our library's policy is that all public programming must be free and open to the public, the library foundation has the option of having fundraising events. Borrowing a great idea from New York Public Library, our foundation hosts an after hours "Literary Lions" dinner at the largest of our branches. Guests are wined and dined among the stacks and have the opportunity to meet some of their favorite authors. If one author is a draw, consider what thirty authors must be.

The Friday night prior to their premiere author event, called Bookmania!, the Martin County Library folk throw a cocktail party at the library called Creative Minds and Creative Cocktails featuring all the authors featured in programs the following day. The authors get to meet and mingle with each other and the public gets to meet and mingle with the authors—for the price of admission. Everyone has a wonderful time, and it's a lovely "mini-fundraiser."

Peruse the Houston Public Library's Web site and you'll find any number of programs that carry the note, "Funded by the Houston Chronicle Book & Author Dinner." This festive event underwritten by the *Houston Chronicle* has put money in the coffers for literacy programs for more than twenty-five years.

Christine Watkins reports in an article in the June 1, 2002, *American Libraries* that Los Angeles Public Library goes the glam route, hosting fifty fundraising dinners featuring authors in fifty private homes all on the same night. Individual ticket prices range from $300 to $2,500 depending on the author of your choice. Many cities have an Arts and Lectures series, which heavily features—you guessed it—authors. I know the series in Seattle is wildly popular, often drawing more than 3,000 people at $25 a pop. Yes, the occasional architect, say, will slip into the lineup, but mostly it is authors, poets and playwrights. So remember, hosting authors can be a money-making experience if that's what you're after.

Authors All Around

Libraries aren't the only agencies that have a stake in the author game. It almost goes without saying that a bookstore's stock in trade is the author visit, and that's exactly the model that publishers are accustomed to dealing with. There are lots of other opportunities out there, however.

I talked earlier about public libraries taking authors into the schools, but schools can and do take the initiative to invite local authors in so that their students can have an opportunity to read a book and then make a personal connection with the person who wrote it. It's a discovery process in many ways for students, not the least of which is that books come from people. Author and librarian Toni Buzzeo seconds the motion. "I was a big reader as kid," she told me, "but I always thought authors were dead." I keep thinking of the four year old who discovers that milk comes from cows and not from the grocery store—same kind of thing. Barbara Carmody, Teen and Education Services Coordinator for King County Library System, recounts one such school appearance: "I saw Jack Gantos hold 800 middle school kids mesmerized for an hour. Students covered the school with posters they had made to welcome him. After the lecture, the kids stormed the school library in order to get a book signed and have a few words with Jack."

Organizations of all stripes benefit from an author visit. Service clubs can enjoy an author who writes on civic or business topics. The Downtown Association may host Paco Underhill, the author of *Why We Buy* and *The Call of the Mall*. I've known Rotary groups that enjoyed a presentation by young lawyer and author Drew Hansen based on his book about Martin Luther King. The Seattle chapter of the Sons of Ireland wanted nothing more than for Malachy McCourt to speak at their luncheon. And Malachy, being the trooper he is, even did an event in a pub.

Savvy businesses plan author events for their employees and as a part of their staff development plan. Microsoft regularly hosts science and technology writers—and, wouldn't you know it, science fiction authors. Expose your employees to the best and the brightest, the thinking is, and stir their creativity. Companies such as SAFECO Insurance, Boeing and Starbucks all have active author events programs. It's a great deal for the employee—how much easier is it to bop down to your company auditorium (on work time!) to hear an author (or log on to the event on the computer at your desk) than to pick yourself up off the couch after a long day and travel somewhere else for an author event. It's a great deal for the company as well. Their employees are exposed to new ideas or experience a multicultural world view, or perhaps they just hear about something good to read. Additionally, it's a nice kind out outreach for the company. Authors hosted by Microsoft or Starbucks may gain a whole new perspective, and respect, for the company.

I often think hospitals are missing a bet by not hosting author events, although I know many have begun educational programs. A talk by a well-known doctor or scientist on health or lifestyle issues just may draw me into a hospital, ordinarily a place I like to avoid at all costs. And once I'm there, I may feel familiar enough to return when I do need those kinds of medical services.

On the other hand, there are places I love to frequent that also benefit from author events. One enterprising author event specialist in Seattle organized a "Cooks and Books" program. A restaurant hosts the evening, the chef cooks a meal from a newly published cookbook, and the author circulates among the diners. Everyone goes home well fed with a signed copy of the book. A chance to meet and eat with Patricia Wells? My husband and I couldn't sign up fast enough. What a nice enticement for me to enjoy great food at a restaurant I might not have previously patronized.

No matter what your company, agency, or interest group, the opportunity to host an author successfully is there. All it takes is a little thought, imagination and organization. And this book, of course, to guide you through the process.

2

Establishing the Basics

Snagging a great author and having a successful author event will come easier with a plan. Anyone you deal with—be it author, agent, publicist, publisher or grantmaker—will want to know exactly what you have in mind for an author event. Virginia Stanley, Library Marketing Director for HarperCollins Publishers, believes that "advance planning and flexibility are key factors for successful author events." So start by brainstorming and answering some basic questions.

Why?

In the previous chapter, I talked a little about the benefits of author events and what motivates some agencies to do them. Now it's time for you to decide on your own unique reasons to stage an author program. Here are some things to think about to get you started:

- I want to put my agency on the map with a big-name author.
- It's my library's mission to provide literary programming.
- I want to reach a particular segment of the community by bringing in an author who would have specific appeal to a group such as teens or seniors.

- There's a lot of community interest in this particular topic or issue. An author would stimulate discussion.

- I want to introduce the readers in my community to books and authors they might not otherwise discover.

- An author visit would support the book group activity in my community.

- I want to foster relationships between my library and the authors who live in the community.

Whatever your reasons turn out to be, think them out and write them down so you'll have a solid foundation for the rest of the process.

Martin County Library in Florida built five new buildings in six years. They decided author events would be a good vehicle to help showcase their new buildings. The highly successful Bookmania! was the result. Bookmania! combines lots of well-known authors with tons of volunteers from the community for a fabulous one-day literary party in the community in terrific library venues.

Novello is a highly regarded literary festival put on by the Public Library of Charlotte and Mecklenberg County in North Carolina. Over sixteen years, Novello grew from a week of events to two solid weeks of literary programming. Dick Pahle, Development Director for PLCMC, says, "I firmly believe that the most fundamental decision to make when exploring/considering an event (or series of events) like our Novello is to 'determine its purpose.' " This festival of reading, he told me, really had two purposes. "During the first decade of its existence (under the leadership of former Library Director Bob Cannon), our festival had a 'stated purpose' and a 'real purpose.'

"The 'stated purpose' was 'it was our gift to the reading community.' It was never intended as a fundraising event. Its stated purpose was 'public service.' The 'real purpose,' however, was not that at all. The real purpose was to elevate the library in the minds of citizens with a highly visible event. To say Bob Cannon didn't care that much about the 'public service' of the event would be an exaggeration.... but his principle objective was to make a big splash for the library. Do something big. Get the community talking. Generate media coverage. Bob was smart enough to know that this would pay dividends down the road."

Your purpose may change as time goes on. That's the case now with Novello. Budgets have tightened, and it got harder and harder for the folks at PLCMC to top themselves year after spectacular year. As Dick observes, "There are only so many John Grishams, Toni Morrisons, and Stephen Kings out there." It's time for PLCMC to determine a new purpose for

Novello. "Once we do that," Dick told me, "all other decisions will be driven by that."

Who?

Once you've decided "why," it's time to turn your attention to "who." Actually, there are three "whos" here. The first two are the author and the audience, and one depends quite a bit on the other. Do you want a best-selling author or a local writer? Do you want an expert in a given field or someone who's at the forefront of a topical concern? This will depend on the audience you expect or hope to attract.

For example, if you're trying to appeal specifically to seniors who have the time and means to travel, you might want to target a travel writer like Rick Steves, who does the *Europe through the Back Door* series. Many folks become interested in genealogy and history after they finally have some leisure time to pursue it. That may account for some of the wild success of books like Tom Brokaw's *The Greatest Generation*. Topical issues such as long-term health care and social security may have an appeal not only to seniors but to us aging baby boomers as well. This is not to say that seniors wouldn't also be interested in broader and more literary topics, just that if you're specifically seeking an older audience, you need to play to the interests of the demographic.

I find that book clubs are a great group for author programming. They are interested in and savvy about what's published and love the thrill of discovering a new author. They are glad to hear from an author like Anita Diamont who penned the book club classic *The Red Tent;* but they may also enjoy hearing from a lesser-known literary light, like Debra Dean, whose first novel, *The Madonnas of Leningrad,* was recently published to great critical acclaim.

I'm sure you've seen the mayhem that happens whenever Harry Potter author J. K. Rowling does an author event. Although the Harry Potter books are a unique force of nature, keep in mind that kids connect to books in a special and significant way. A small library in our system had 600 children show up to hear and see fantasy author Brian Jacques. Northwest author Peg Kehret's books (*Cages, Nightmare Mountain,* and *Earthquake Terror*) have won just about every state "children's choice" award going. She is especially popular in this area, and her book events are always well attended.

The author you decide to shoot for will depend on who is in your community and who you hope to attract to an event. If you're just starting out with author programming, this may seem like an impossible call to make. How will you know who will come until the actual event? I urge you to gather all the information you can and make an educated guess.

How to educate yourself to make a guess? Look at the demographics in your community. If you're in a downtown core, you might draw young professionals to hear the author of *Freakonomics* or working women to hear Barbara Stanny's financial advice in *Overcoming Underearning*. If your library is awash in teens, consider the author of a graphic novel or a popular teen novelist like Chris Crutcher.

You might want to chat with bookstore owners in your town to learn their take on community interests. Often local bookstores will have their own local best-seller list. Such a list might give you lots of ideas about what authors and topics would be popular.

Make a little study of what's currently going on in your community. It will tell you what market niches you don't have to fill or give you a good idea of audiences you can build on. We have a burgeoning arts scene in our community that is beginning to set itself apart from the nearby city of Seattle. There's a museum, dance company and theatre company, and there are plans afoot to build a new performing arts center. There's also a gentleman in our neck of the woods who does very popular opera preview programming. Norm preps his audience of opera-goers by giving a history of the opera, talking a little about the plot and who's who in the cast and playing musical excerpts of the highlights. Norm's audiences are absolutely devoted. When Joseph Volpe became available to us on his book tour promoting *The Toughest Show on Earth,* a memoir of his years as Director of the Metropolitan Opera, we immediately thought of Norm. Norm volunteered his time to interview Mr. Volpe about his book, and the arts community turned out en masse. We correctly pinpointed a demographic and tied into an existing audience. The publisher was pleased that we gave this program a different twist; Mr. Volpe was pleased with the change of pace and to have the chance to chat with someone as knowledgeable as Norm. It was a win-win-win event.

So look hard and long at you're community and see how your author event fits in. Whoever you are dealing with to set up the event—author, publisher or agent—will want to know.

HarperCollins's Virginia Stanley created a tip sheet for librarians hoping to do author events. Here's her advice about author selection: "While it's difficult to predict audience size, it's necessary to have a general idea of how many people you expect at your event. If you have a proven track record of getting large crowds to attend your author programs, you'll have an advantage in securing an author. "Big name" authors are accustomed to speaking to several hundred people at one time, so please set realistic goals.

Also, consider the size of your meeting room. A large venue offers the opportunity to host a big name author, while smaller rooms are good for first novelists and mid-list authors. It's a good idea to provide us with a wish list of authors—as oftentimes, your first choice may not be available."

The third "who" has to do with planning and producing the event. Who will be on your team? Are you flying solo on this event, or will you have a committee? Will other organizations be involved? Who will be responsible for what aspects of the event? More about this later.

What?

Now think about what kind of event this will be. In the HarperCollins tip sheet I referred to earlier, Virginia asks the questions publishers want to know:

- When?
- Where?
- What time?
- Who's attending?
- Is this a panel?
- Is this a special event?
- Is this part of a monthly series?
- How will the event be structured?
- Will this be in a special venue?

Virginia rightly says, "The more information you can provide us, the better."

Are you thinking of a big, fancy fundraising dinner? An author reading with Q&A to follow? Will someone interview the author? Will it be an interactive session with the speaker? Will it be a panel discussion of authors? (I've always wanted to do a panel of Northwest mystery writers.) Is this event part of a series? If so, who else is in the series? Does it happen weekly, monthly or quarterly? Does the venue remain the same? I've long admired the ingenuity of a small music ensemble that presents its concerts in a variety of interesting places—a local art gallery, the lobby of a museum, glass artist Dale Chihuly's workshop.

We once did high tea with the "Queen of Romantic Suspense," Mary Higgins Clark, and that was great fun. Just recently a local library did an adult spelling bee featuring ten teams of three spellers each in the competition. Who picked out the spelling words? It was none other than Anu Garg, the author of *A Word a Day: A Romp through Some of the Most Unusual and Intriguing Words in English.* The event was well attended, got tons of press, highlighted the author and the library and raised money for literacy. Not only that, everyone had a good time. Sharon Fiffer writes mysteries featuring "antiques picker" Jane Wheel, who is particularly fond of Bakelite. The Evanston Public Library parlayed this into a program featuring Sharon and an antiques dealer with her prized pieces of—you guessed it—Bakelite.

Publishers and authors are always looking for fun and creative events, so whatever you can do to make your event a little bit different will help. I know a local bookseller who arranged a hip singles evening event for *Sex and the City* author Candace Bushnell in a trendy bar. Alas, libraries can't be quite *that* flexible. Or can they?

Where?

Where is this event going to take place? In your library meeting room? In your hospital auditorium? In your local theatre? In your school gym? If your organization doesn't have a good spot, consider partnering with an agency that does. (There's lots more about partnering in the next chapter.) When planning where to hold the event, you'll need to think about availability, cost and capacity. How many people do you expect to come? What kind of atmosphere do you want to create? It's interesting that an author in a high school multipurpose room can make you feel like you're late to geometry class whereas the same author in a professional theatrical venue with proper mood lighting can make you feel like you're out for a night on the town. Don't be afraid to underestimate the capacity you need. Remember that a lot of people in a smaller space create excitement and a sense of privilege whereas a few people in a large space feel awkward.

When?

Whenever one of my programming librarians comes to me with concerns about too many people attending an event, my response is always, "Let's *hope* we have that problem." Again, your audience and your location are going to determine the day, time and season or time of year for your event. Will you hold your event in the evening? After school? Saturday morning? Sunday afternoon? Just before the holiday season hits?

Commuters may not reemerge from their homes to go to a program at 7 or 7:30 P.M., but they may stop in on the way home from work at 5 or 5:30 P.M. If you schedule an event on a Saturday morning in a suburban community, you may be fighting with soccer games and grocery shopping, but Sunday afternoon might tie in nicely to family time at the library. In our community, we've had to work hard to fill a room for an evening program. Recently we experimented and hosted Joanne Harris at 12:30 on a weekday. The place was packed. It might have been the lure of *Chocolat* that called 120 people to the library on a Thursday afternoon, but we were delighted. We saw older folks who don't care to drive at night, some young professionals who dashed over from the downtown office buildings and a few stay-at-home moms with babes at breast. (That ticked off the older folks, but that's another story.) The audience applauded and cheered when we asked them if we should schedule more events during the day. With that success under our belt, we scheduled Marian Keyes for a lunchtime event. The room was filled with hip chicks of all ages giggling like mad at Marian's observations.

How?

Okay. You've got your author event well fleshed out. You know why you're doing it, you've targeted your audience and you know when and where it will be. You've chosen your work team members. Now, how, specifically, is all of this going to get done? Who is responsible for what portions of the event? Who will make the final decisions? Will you need to recruit volunteers? Who will do that task? Are you going to issue tickets for this event, or is it first come, first served? If you're doing tickets, how will they be distributed? Who is going to be at the other end of that contact number? Who will be selling the books? (Bear in mind, book sales are mandatory for author events.) And then there's the ancillary question to HOW? Which is—

How Much?

How will this event be paid for? Who is going to prepare and birddog the budget? Are you hoping to snag a grant or enlist the aid of a corporate sponsor? Who will do that research and write the proposal? (Check the appendix for a sample proposal for corporate sponsorship.) Who will do the follow up paperwork? Are you charging admission? How will you determine the price?

You'll find that you need to know what your budget is before you go off on your author hunt. As Virginia Stanley says, "Sending authors to events can be costly. Transportation, accommodations and other local expenses add up." Authors may or may not require an honorarium. You need to know what you can afford before you begin negotiations.

So it's matter of all those journalistic standbys: Why? Who? What? Where? When? How? (And How Much?). It's a lot to consider, but they pay off in the long run. Read on for lots more details about all of these components so you can truly flesh out the details of your event. Knowing your purpose and having a plan is the foundation of both securing an author and ensuring a successful event.

3

Cooperate and Conquer

Putting on an author event may seem like an overwhelming task. Before you holler uncle, remember that you don't need to be in this alone. As a matter of fact, you might be better off if you're not. A partner in crime can spread the wealth—and the work.

Think about whom you might partner with in the community. Here are some thoughts and examples.

Bookstores

It might seem like libraries and bookstores are in a competitive relationship, but truly, they have a lot to offer one another. Bookstores often have the inside track with publishers in snagging authors who are on book tour. Your local bookstore might be your best pal in rounding up an author. In addition, bookstores can often request money from the publisher for advertising to which libraries don't have access. (Grrrrr.) On the other hand, libraries typically have meeting rooms, while many bookstores do not. Librarians are more likely to go out into the community to booktalk or give a presentation to community groups. Booksellers don't usually function in that way.

Your clientele may overlap a little, but the odds are if you put your flyers in the library and the bookstore you'll reach two different audiences. Sometimes the bookstore is the touchstone for local book groups, sometimes the library is. If you cooperate, your bases are covered. I think it works better to co-develop an event with a bookstore rather than ask them just to sell at an event. There's something about the involvement that makes things run more smoothly. Too often when we've asked a bookseller to come and sell for an author event without involving them in the planning, problems would arise. Like they wouldn't show up. That's a problem.

If you involve a bookstore, your selling problems are basically solved. The bookstore will take care of it; bringing the books, the bags, the cash registers, the change, the credit card swipes and the booksellers. Some bookstores will even give you a cut of the take. Personally, I'm just happy to have them handle it. It's one less thing for me to worry about.

We had a happy association with an independent Seattle bookseller for many years. Working with a different bookseller in every town wasn't working out for us—as noted previously. So instead we had one bookseller do the sales for every appearance. We'd book authors in our far-flung branches throughout the county, and Chauni would sell the books at each event. Sometimes we had six people show up. Sometimes we had 300. Chauni was always there. Now that I think on it, beatification is probably in order.

One of my favorite joint ventures with a bookstore took place in a tiny town in the south part of King County. Bob has a great, old-timey, quirky bookstore, complete with easy chairs and a wood stove, well used and loved by the community. In this case the typical roles were reversed. Bob had just finished an addition to his historic old building and had not yet put bookshelves in it—just the place to set up chairs for a program. The library, on the other hand, was tiny and had no meeting room. I was setting up a library tour for the irrepressible Malachy McCourt and was glad to bring him to town—and Malachy, trouper that he is, was glad to come. The Friends of the Library dove into the project with abandon making arrangements for refreshments and decorations. The library was able to churn out flyers that would have been problematic for Bob to underwrite. Word of mouth was great. Between the library staff, the Friends of the Library and Bob's customers, the whole town knew about the event.

Malachy and I pulled into town and stopped at the one restaurant for a bite before the program. By the time we were finished, the rest of the diners had disappeared. "Where is everybody?!" inquired Malachy as we were preparing to leave. "Oh!" our waitress said, quite excited, "Everyone's gone to the book signing." And indeed they had. When we walked in the front door of the bookstore, the place was jammed. The place was decorated to the gills, an Irish harpist was playing, there was a fire in the potbelly stove, hot cider was simmering away and the Friends of the Library had clearly baked themselves silly for days to produce a vast spread of cookies and sweets. Malachy was charmed, and so was I. Nearly two hundred people had packed themselves into this neighborhood bookstore in this small town to hear an author speak. Said Bob happily, referring to the building's past life as a tavern, "There haven't been this many people in this building since they served beer!"

We currently have a terrific cooperative relationship with one of our local independent bookstores. Even though it's a good-sized bookstore, they drool when they hear that we get an average of 3,000 people through our doors each day. They not only sell books at our author events but treat the programs as their own, promoting them in the store and in their own events calendar.

Libraries

Bookstores aren't the only cooperative game in town. Perhaps you can share an author (and the costs) with another library. The folks who do the Arts and Lectures series in major towns are old pros at this. I've noticed that the authors who appear in Seattle to do a lecture often appear soon after in Portland, Oregon, in the same kind of venue. Portland is a three-hour drive or a twenty-minute flight from Seattle, so it makes sense. Sometimes I see that San Francisco is tied into this chain as well.

We've had good luck cooperating with sister library systems on author events. Kitsap County is a thirty-five-minute ferry ride from King County. Kitsap Regional Library has a well-crafted countywide author event called Kitsap Reads that draws great audiences. Whenever Martha, the event planner for Kitsap, or I would get a line on a hot author, we'd call the other to see if we could make our schedules coincide. Clearly this takes some advance planning, but it's a great investment of time. The author gets double the exposure for the price of a ferry ride and, perhaps, an extra night in a hotel. Publishers and publicists love this. It's such a short distance away yet neither our media markets nor our audiences overlap. What's not to like?

If you choose to try such a venture, I'd urge you not to get hung up on a straight fifty-fifty split of expenses. Be creative and cater to each other's strengths and resources. One library might not have much cash but may have great connections to publishers or have a great hotel or B&B that's willing to comp a room. However you work it out, remember that the strength of your double proposal is likely to have a greater appeal to a publisher and give you a greater chance of success snagging a terrific author.

The logistics of asking a publisher for an author on behalf of two entities might seem daunting, but it's really not so bad. Here's a sample proposal submitted on behalf of King County Library System and Kitsap Regional Library:

Library Appearance Proposal for Alice Walker

King County Library System	Kitsap Regional Library
960 Newport Way NW	1301 Sylvan Way
Issaquah, WA 98027	Bremerton, WA 98310
Library Programming Contact:	Chapple Langemack,
e-mail: chaplang@kcls.org	425.369.3318

In response the request for "large, off-site proposals," this cooperative library venture would give Alice Walker two appearances with guaranteed large, lively and appreciative audiences in two distinct markets in the Puget Sound area, often overlooked by event planners. Library staff escorts can offer seamless transportation to each venue.

Event Dates: Whenever author and venues are mutually available.

Event Time: Prefer evening—7:30 P.M.

Event Format: Remarks/Reading, followed by Q&A. Sales will be provided on site by local independent bookstores.

Audience: Adults and older teens with particular emphasis on book club members. We anticipate 600–700 at both venues.

KCLS Venue: The gorgeous 402-seat Kirkland Performance Center adjacent to the Kirkland Library.

KRL Venue: Venue on Bainbridge Island to be determined.

King County Library System: The fourth largest public library in the United States, KCLS has a history of successful author events. We recently welcomed overflow crowds to an evening with Tom Robbins. Events at the Kirkland Performance Center tap a well-heeled, well-educated audience who prefer not to "cross the bridge" to Seattle and strongly support Eastside author and cultural events.

Event Co-Sponsors: Park Place Books and the Kirkland Performance Center.

Kitsap Regional Library: sponsors the popular Kitsap Reads author series. Bainbridge Island is a vibrant arts community, home to more than 200 published authors. Bainbridge audiences embrace author events that they don't have to travel to Seattle to attend.

Event Co-Sponsors: The Kitsap Regional Library Foundation, the local newspaper *The Sun* and the Independent Booksellers of Westsound.

Publicity: KCLS will distribute 8,000 brochures through 42 community library sites, posters, flyers and e-mail notification to our "author alert" list of 1,000 people who have asked to be notified of upcoming author visits. Direct mail notification will go out to 5,000 adults participating in our "Reading Rewards" program. New releases will be sent to all newspapers in the area, and radio and television stations will be contacted. This author appearance will be featured on our Web site (http://www.kcls.org), which receives more than nine million hits per month.

Kitsap Regional Library heavily markets author events through the local newspaper, libraries, the library Web site (http://www. krl.org), bookstores and cable-access TV.

Past authors at KCLS events: Robert Hass, Malachy McCourt, Joyce Carol Oates, Rick Bragg, Jacquelyn Mitchard, Nikki Giovanni, Mark Salzman, Molly Gloss, Ha Jin, David James Duncan, Lisa Scottoline, Susan Isaacs, David Rakoff, Mary Higgins Clark, Laurie R. King, Elizabeth George, Robert Pinsky and Adriana Trigiani have all spoken at the King County Library System.

Past authors at KRL events: Past authors in this series include Rick Bragg, Ursula LeGuin, Molly Gloss, Nuala O'Faolain and Sherman Alexie.

Schools and Colleges

I know you have schools in your community, and you might also have a university or community college. They are all fertile territory for cooperative book events.

King County Library System often brings children's and young adult authors into the schools. It's a win-win situation. The public library may have more time, connections and resources than a school to track down an author. But the school has that lovely enticement—a built in audience. Publishers are guaranteed exposure—as is the public library. And it's a lot easier to get one author to a school than it is to get hundreds of kids into the library. Just make sure you have a public librarian on the scene and that there's a banner with your library's name on it prominently displayed, and you're set.

For several years our library's teen librarian took author Ji-Li Jiang to visit selected schools. Ji-Li talked about her book *Red Scarf Girl* and about her experiences growing up during the Cultural Revolution. The kids were fascinated, the teachers were thrilled and we were delighted. This event became a little too successful when Ji-Li's appearance was written into the curriculum with the assumption the library would fund the event each year. But that's another story.

Remember that there isn't any reason that you can't do both. We serve a large county, so we may choose to do a program with an author at a school at one end of the county and a public event at a branch library at the other end. This way you have the guaranteed school audience and parents and other community members have a chance at seeing a well-known author. This is exactly what we do with our signature author event for teens, the Kim Lafferty Lecture. I asked Debbie Schneider, Public Programming Coordinator for King County Library System, to outline this event:

The Kim series highlights a young adult author who has created a substantial body of work. The authors have included Chris Crutcher, Will Hobbs, Tamora Pierce, Jack Gantos and Gordon Korman. This has become one of our most well-attended teen events, because of the cooperative effort we've managed to devise.

We've worked with the Washington Library Media Association for several years in planning the event, because they contract to bring an author to their conference in October. This alone reduces the cost of the programs—because they pay for part of the transportation to the Seattle area.

The next step is to find a central location in our county for the daytime programs. We've had a long-standing cooperative arrangement with a local performance center, which allows us to use the facility at no cost if it is not scheduled. This 403-seat theater is centrally located, has good parking and is next door to one of our larger libraries. A daytime author event can draw bused students from area schools, maximizing the potential audience. Teachers are contacted in the spring so they can reserve seats for the event in advance. This allows the teachers to incorporate the reading of the author's books into their curriculum for fall.

For the second program of the day, we usually work with a school in the more southern part of the county. Many recently renovated or newly built schools have excellent theaters or performing arts centers. We pay a small fee for the use of such facilities, but all technical services are included and they even arrange for ushers. Again, students are bused to this central venue for the author event.

With this structure we've been able to offer author events to an audience of as many as 1,200 students in one day. It maximizes the potential audience while keeping the costs of the event manageable and this process cements relationships with teachers in the library service area.

Anatomy of a Joint Effort

Another collaboration in our community was borne of the fabled "Seattle Reads" project launched by the Washington Center for the Book. Our local community college took that model and applied it to their campus. The college chose the book *Longitude* by Dava Sobel with the thought that it could be taught in some way in across the curriculum. Every student read the book and studied it in different ways in all of their classes. English classes read the book as literature. Math and science classes focused on the technical aspects of the book. Geography and history classes took their lesson plans from those aspects of the work. Toward the end of the quarter, the author was brought in to speak to the student body. In the second year of this project the college administrators sought to open up this effort to the community to expand its audience base (and funding potential).

The library signed on to cooperate. Choosing a book that met the needs of the community college *and* appealed to the general reading public was a big challenge. Connie was the public librarian tapped to sit in on the selection committee, which consisted of professors from various disciplines, plus a college librarian. Here's Connie's description of the process:

We began the process of choosing the book in the winter so that we'd be ready for a fall start. If this sounds like months of reading and attending meetings, that's precisely correct. We started by generating a long list of books. Each member then read one or two of the books on the list and made a recommendation to the group to either delete the book or keep it in consideration. Each successive meeting saw a shorter list, more members reading each book, and more lively discussions.

As a public librarian and a long-time book club member, I started searching for that perfect book that would grab the students and make them all into lifelong readers and book club members. I also wanted a book that I could recommend without reservation to our patrons and to the books clubs that I work with. I soon realized that my choice might not be the perfect book for the program, because applicability to diverse curriculum areas was a crucial criterion that a book needed to meet. Finding books that would integrate the humanities with as many other areas of study as possible proved to be quite a challenge.

All of the committee members read the final four or five books, and we were able to come to a consensus on the final selection. One of our criteria that came into play during the final selection was if the author was a good speaker and if he or she was likely to be available during the course of the program.

Our choice for this year, The Botany of Desire by Michael Pollan, relates to a large number of curriculum areas and also happens to be about several agricultural products that are important here in the Pacific Northwest: apples, tulips, and potatoes. It will be interesting to see how the book is used on the campus and in the community as the year progresses. Personally, I'm hoping for a multicultural potato festival involving lots of melted butter!

With the book selected, program planning can begin. Lisa, the program coordinator for our library, met with the Director of the Liberal Arts Program at the community college to discuss the possibilities. Says Lisa, "We considered both the form and the content of programs to present a well-rounded series that will have broad appeal and support the book in a variety of ways. The partnership gives us access to scholars to facilitate discussions and another agency to share the cost of bringing the author in for appearances both on campus and in the public library."

I'm glad to report that this is a program that has gained popularity and community involvement. Our most recent choice, *The Things They Carried* by Tim O'Brien, has spawned proposals for programs featuring local Vietnam veterans and a request to host the traveling Vietnam Memorial in the park next door.

Arts Organizations

Is there a museum or theatre in town that you can cooperate with? They may have things to offer that will expand the scope or appeal of your program.

For instance, our library system lacks large meeting room spaces. Two hundred is about the most we can squeeze into any given room, and even then the fire department is not amused. When a really big author comes to town, we just plain need more room. The performing arts center next to one of our libraries proved to be the perfect answer. This gorgeous 400-seat hall gave us room for a hefty audience but still had an intimate feel. The theatre manager was more than happy to give us the use of the theatre in exchange for the exposure. We were glad for them to add our author to their "bill of fare," exposing us to their audiences. It was a great deal for both of us—no venue expenses for us, no author expenses for them, and we both benefited.

The Washington Center for the Book at the Seattle Public Library cooperated with an arts organization in a different way. When Julie Otsuka came to town for Seattle Reads, Chris Higashi and her crew expanded the program by offering complementary programming. She arranged for four free performances by The 5th Avenue Theatre's Adventure Musical Theatre Touring Company of an original musical based on Ken Mochizuki's award-winning picture book *Baseball Saved Us,* another literary work that touches on the Japanese internment. This musical had toured to dozens of schools but had not been presented for the general public. Audiences included children and families, seniors, and everyone in between. Mr. Mochizuki joined the cast for a post-performance discussion with the audience.

The Tacoma Public Library began a happy partnership with the local children's museum. The museum got a national grant to create an interactive exhibit to promote literacy using children's book illustrations. It turns out they didn't have enough room to host all of the artwork. Enter the library with exhibit space. The next year the library joined the team earlier in the process and suggested the artwork of Gerald McDermott for the project. The museum couldn't quite afford to bring out Mr. McDermott for a consulting trip. The library was able to snare a grant from the local Junior League so that the illustrator was able to come out and consult with the museum on exhibit design and do public programs and school visits for the library. When the exhibit is complete, Gerald McDermott will return to do more school visits and public programs for the library and appearances for the museum. Says David Domkoski, the TPL staff member who masterminded this cooperative venture, "Any time you can cross-pollinate and cross-promote for an event, you are well ahead of the game."

Each year our library hosts an event for book club members through-out the country. It's a half day that features booktalks, a mini-workshop on an area of concern to book groups, and, the pièce de résistance, a presentation by an author. Our most recent gathering featured the author Debra Dean. We were inspired by the world of art in Debra's book, *The Madonnas of Leningrad,* to use art as a central theme for our day. Our librarians booktalked other books that revolved around art and artists (I can feel you librarians going into list mode—*The Sixteen Pleasures, Girl in Hyacinth Blue, Johanna, Girl with a Pear Earring* ...). Wanting to involve the local art museum in some way, we invited the curator to speak briefly to our group about the museum. Not only did Michael describe the current offerings of the museum, he spoke brilliantly about the process of opening yourself up to art, whether it's the book your book club is reading or a piece of art in a museum. He inspired us all to go beyond making a judgment about what we like or don't like and make a true effort to see what the artist or writer is trying to tell us. It was a terrific addition to the program, and perhaps the beginning of even more cooperative ventures between these two organizations.

Community Groups

A humble but no less effective cooperative venture involves a local community group. Our local gardening club loves to cosponsor garden writers with the library. One month it might be a recent work by a local author on the joys of begonias. Another time it might be Ann Lovejoy, who in the Northwest is a gardening rock star. The program has a built-in base audience—the garden club members—and is open to any interested members of the public. We split the honorarium for the author. Everybody wins.

So think about who's in your community—or a short drive away—that you might partner with. Perhaps it's a church, a historical society, the chamber of commerce or women's business group. Jack Canfield, of "Chicken Soup" fame, also writes motivational books on business success. When *The Success Principles* came out, the local Chamber of Commerce could not have been happier to have him as a luncheon speaker. Six hundred business folk turned out to be inspired by Jack's techniques. What a great thing to have the library connected to the business community in such a tangible way.

So think about the service clubs and nonprofit groups and maybe even the big companies in town when you are planning your author events. One of these potential partners might be able to provide that one extra thing that makes the program feasible.

4

Authors, Authors Everywhere

Once you're all geared up for an author program, you're ready for the key ingredient—and the fun part—authors. Where do you find them? How do you approach them? Do you pay them? How much? Have patience. All will be revealed in this and the following chapters.

There are several ways to snag authors—contacting them yourself, working through a publisher, working through an agent or working with an arts or cultural organization that acts as a clearinghouse. Which you choose depends on how much time, money, persistence and flexibility you have. If you choose to do a lot of author programming, you may use all four channels.

Doing It Yourself

The search for an author can be as easy as picking up the morning paper or doing a quick Internet search. These days many authors have their own Web site. If you take look at LisaScottoline.com, for instance, you'll see Lisa's availability and tour schedule. Sometimes you can request an appearance via the Web site. Sometimes there'll be a name and phone number or e-mail of the person at the publishing house who handles such requests.

Or there may be contact information for the author's agent. That's a good clue as to how that author likes to do business.

While you're online you can check out such sites as the one developed by Poets & Writers, Inc. This group maintains a directory that gives contact information for more than 7,400 contemporary poets, fiction writers and performance writers. You'll find it at www.pw.org/directry/. Another good site to browse for potential authors is Authors on the Web: www.authorsontheweb.com. This Web site is a product of the folks who produce bookreporter.com. It lists forthcoming and recent releases, author roundtables and links to many author Web sites.

Another Web source is Authors @ Your Library. The Association of American Publishers, in partnership with the American Library Association, Friends of Libraries U.S.A. (FOLUSA) and *Library Journal,* developed a free online matchmaking service that links publishers and librarians. Librarians responsible for event planning can search for authors and for information about publishers and their imprints. The idea is to let publishers identify opportunities for author events at libraries and simplify the search for librarians. You can check it out online at www.authorsatyourlibrary.org. HarperCollins Publishers has launched a speakers bureau to provide information on authors (published by HarperCollins, naturally) who may be available. That Web site is www.harpercollinsspearsbureau.com.

Don't forget to try the old-fashioned way while you're researching. I know authors who are in the phone book. If you know where he or she lives, you're set. Check out the book's dust jacket for clues. For many years, our State Library produced a list of Washington authors with listings of their recent work. Is there a local writer's group in your area? That might be a good source of information as well. In our area, there are very active local writer's groups, a regional writer's organization and a local chapter of the Society of Children's Book Authors and Illustrators. You can check out that national Web site at http://www.scbwi.org/ and search for your local chapter.

Keep your eyes open. Watch the newspaper. Read *Library Journal, Publisher's Weekly* and other such publications. Canny Judy, who runs that terrific author event program in Utah, keeps a dossier on each author whom she is interested in hosting. It not only helps her track the person down, it gives her an idea of the kind of event that might interest him or her. More on Judy's clever tips later.

Working through a Publisher

Every author is assigned a publicist within his publishing company. A publicist for a big publisher like HarperCollins may have fifteen or twenty authors assigned to her, all with books coming out the next publishing season. Smaller publishing houses may have a publicity director, period. The publicist may be the logical place for you to start your process. She's the one who knows the author's strengths and preferences. She puts together the book tour.

The Ins and Outs of a Book Tour

What's a book tour? You've seen it action, you just might not have known it at the time. When you see Jane Fonda on a morning TV talk show or on *Larry King Live* chatting about her recent autobiography, that's part of her book tour. She'll go from city to city, appearing on radio and television and making personal appearances at bookstores to sell her book. And because Jane has a really good publicist—or more likely, several really good publicists—as soon as the book tour activity subsides, the promotion for her new movie begins.

When you are a stop on an author's book tour, it's at the publisher's expense, not yours. But in order to be a stop on a book tour you have to convince the publicist that your program will be easy to get to, interesting for the author, noticed by the news media and well attended—preferably by rabid book buyers who will purchase copies for autographing at your event.

When I first starting doing author visits, I thought that book tours were somehow geographically linear. I assumed a Seattle author, say, Rebecca Wells of *Divine Secrets of the Ya Ya Sisterhood* fame, would begin her tour in Seattle then travel along the west coast to Portland, San Francisco and Los Angeles. From LA, I imagined she would hop over to Phoenix or Denver or Dallas, go on to Florida and up the East Coast to New York and then stop in Chicago or Minneapolis on her way home to Seattle. Boy, was I wrong. Author tours have absolutely nothing to do with geography—or logic for that matter. I heard science fiction author Greg Bear joke that authors have a terrible time traveling after September 11—disheveled individuals with a fistful of one-way tickets are very suspect.

Want to see what an author's life on tour is like? Here's the schedule for Joanne Harris's latest visit from England:

Thursday, January 12
FREEHOLD, NJ
Barnes & Noble
Freehold, NJ
7 P.M.

Friday, January 13
FAIRFIELD, CT
Borders
Fairfield, CT
7 P.M.

Sunday, January 15
CORTE MADERA, CA
Book Passage
Corte Madera, CA
1 P.M.

Monday, January 16
SAN FRANCISO, CA
Books Inc.
Laurel Village Store
San Francisco, CA
7 P.M.

Tuesday, January 17
SPOKANE, WA
Auntie's Bookstore
Spokane, WA
7:30 P.M.

Wednesday, January 18
SEATTLE, WA
University Bookstore Presents at

Seattle Public Library
Seattle, WA
7 P.M.

Thursday, January 19
BELLEVUE, WA
Bellevue Regional Library
King County Library System
Bellevue, WA
12:30 P.M.

LAKE FOREST PARK, WA
Third Place Books
Lake Forest Park, WA
7 P.M.

Friday, January 20
PHOENIX, AZ
Poisoned Pen
Scottsdale, AZ
7 P.M.

Sunday, January 22
HOUSTON, TX
Murder by the Book
Houston, TX
1 P.M.

Monday, January 23
SAN ANTONIO, TX
Twig Book Shop
San Antonio, TX
5 P.M.

And that doesn't include the media and nonpublic events that probably went on—like radio interviews and lunch with librarians at their national conference in San Antonio. I don't know about you, but I'm pooped just reading it.

Understand that the publicist has probably been doing this for some time and has her own contacts and preferences in each city. If you are going to muscle into the tour, you have to muscle someone else out. This makes it doubly important that you have your ducks in a row and can give a cogent case for why your venue is ideal.

The downside of book tours is that they don't always happen when you want them to. If you need J. A. Jance in March and her next book doesn't come out until August, then you need to seek another route. The other thing to keep in mind about book tours is that they can change, often with very little notice. If you're not in a position to fall back and punt if you have to, then a book tour is probably not for you.

Sad but True: A Melodrama

Act One

Setting: A library manager's office in the greater Puget Sound area

Time: Now

Hot white light comes up on library manager sitting at desk, reviewing publicity for upcoming author event. The phone rings.

Manager: (Answers phone distractedly.) Hello.

Voice on Phone: Hello, Ms. Langemack? This is Walter Warren, the publicist for Arthur Author. Arthur is due to be at your library in two weeks, but we've decided to cancel the West Coast part of the book tour. Arthur has had a terrible case of writer's block, you see, but now the words are flowing and we really feel that he needs to stay home and write.

Manager: (Looks stunned. Lips move but no sound emerges.) Fade to black as screams begin.

Finding Ms. Right

Publishers, for some reason, don't always think of libraries when they think of venues for their authors. This drives the library community wild. Hopefully we're making progress in convincing them otherwise. There are some notable exceptions, however. Some publishers, like HarperCollins and Random House, are enlightened enough to have people assigned to the library market. (Note: the HarperCollins Speakers Bureau that I mentioned earlier is a completely different entity from the library marketing department.) If you're in a library, a publisher's library marketing specialist should be your best friend. You should send them champagne, roses and chocolate on a regular basis. They understand how libraries work and fight to represent you to publicists, authors and sales folk. They can give you the lowdown on which authors are likely to meet your needs and those that probably won't. They even know which authors have a soft spot for libraries and prefer such a venue.

So here's a list of your new best friends. The next time you go to a national library conference, stop by the booth and say howdy.

Publishing Industry Contacts

Algonquin Books/Workman Press
www.workman.com
708 Broadway, New York, NY 10003
Contact Name: Ina Stern
Phone: (919) 933.0272
E-mail: ina@algonquin.com

Arte Publico Press
www.artepublicopress.com
4800 Calhoun, Houston, TX 77204
Contact name: Carmen Pena Abrego
Phone: (713) 743.2999
Fax: (713) 743.3080
E-mail: carpen@uh.edu

Capital Books
www.capital-books.com
22841 Quicksilver Drive
Dulles, VA 20166
Contact: Jennifer Hughes
Phone: (703) 661-1533
Fax: (703) 661-1547
E-mail: Jennifer@Booksintl.com

HarperCollins

www.harpercollins.com—publisher's general Web site
www.harperlibrary.com—specific to librarians' needs
10 East 53rd Street
New York, NY 10022
Contact Name: Virginia Stanley
Phone: (212) 207.7592
Fax: (212) 207.6955
E-mail: Virginia.Stanley@harpercollins.com

Other Press

www.otherpress.com
2 Park Avenue, 24th Floor
New York, NY 10022
Contact: Publicity Department
Fax: (212) 414.0939
E-mail: publicity@otherpress.com

Penguin Group USA

www.penguingroup.com
375 Hudson Street
New York, NY 10014-3657
Contact Name: Heather Hart
Phone: (212) 366.2378
Fax: (212) 366.2933
E-mail: Heather.Hart@us.penguingroup.com

Random House

www.randomhouse.com
1745 Broadway, 6-2
New York, NY 10019
Contact Name: Courtney Russell
Phone: (212) 572.2867
Fax: (212) 940.7381
E-mail: Courtney.Russell@randomhouse.com

Simon & Schuster

Atria Books and Washington Square Press
www.simonsays.com
1230 Avenue of the Americas, 13th Floor
New York, NY 10020
Contact Name: Kim Curtain
Phone: (212) 698.7649
Fax: (212) 632.8083
E-mail: kimberly.curtain@simonandschuster.com

St. Martin's Press
www.stmartins.com
175 Fifth Avenue, Suite 1503
New York, NY 10010
Contact Name: Harriet Seltzer
Phone: (212) 674.5151, extension 580
Fax: (212) 674.6132

Be smart about this and lay the groundwork. Give a publisher's representative a good snapshot of your library, your audience and your program. Don't call on Friday afternoon and ask for John Grisham the following week.

Here's a list for librarians considering working with a publishing house to host an author devised by Marcia Lane Purcell, Vice President and Director of Library and Academic Marketing for the Random House. Besides being one of the most charming people on earth, Marcia is one of the foremost supporters of author events in libraries. So when Marcia says do it this way, she knows what she's talking about.

Tips for Booking an Author (From the Publisher's Viewpoint)

1. Plan as far in advance as possible (6 months is reasonable).

2. Put the request in writing and give all known details: name of the sponsoring organization, location of event, date, time, anticipated size/age/makeup of audience, name of contact person, and so on.

3. State the exact nature of the event and the author's participation in it: book and author lunch, breakfast or dinner; lecture; school class(es); conference address/panel, with other authors or alone; length of the presentation; question-and-answer period; theme of the event, author's particular topic; and so on.

4. DO NOT ASK FOR THE MOST FAMOUS AUTHOR OF THE MOMENT!!! Consider local talent, first novelists, mid-list, genre, backlist, self-help, and how-to authors.

5. Request several authors in order of preference. (Make sure they are actually published by the company from which you've requested them!)

6. Be up front and specific about expenses you can cover (or not). This includes speaker's fees, transportation, hotel, meal costs. Try to take advantage of publisher's tours where at least some of these costs are covered.

7. Say if you will have an autographing opportunity and sell books; state who will handle this: the library or school, the Friends or PTA, a local bookstore. Find out how to get the books from the publisher or wholesaler. Books should be on hand well in advance of the event.

8. Once the author has said "yes," confirm all arrangements and agreements with a follow-up letter. Putting details in writing eliminates later confusion.

9. Make the trip as worthwhile as possible from the author's and publisher's point of view: get all the staff informed and involved; educate your audience in advance with flyers, booklists, and other items; try to set up other appearances at the local bookstore, local radio, TV, newspaper. Give the publisher credit by using its name in all PR items.

10. After your successful event, follow-up with a thank you and report to the author and publisher.

Remember that it's in a publisher's interest to help you make your event a success. They can send you photos and sample press releases, posters, bookmarks and sometimes even T-shirts or book bags to help you promote the program.

Working with Agents

The third way I know of to get an author is through a speaker's agent. The agent guarantees the author of your choice for a given date and takes care of all of the transportation and lodging details. You must sign a contract and pay a fee plus travel expenses. It's pricey to book an author through an agent, but it is also the most reliable method. If you're dealing with an individual author, he may forget or change his mind at the last moment. Book tours, as I mentioned previously, are notorious for "flexing" en route. If you absolutely, positively must have an author on a certain date, this may be the way to go.

Steven Barclay runs an agency awash with literary talent that you've probably heard on National Public Radio. Steven has also had a lot of experience working with libraries. I asked him for his advice to librarians on working with an agent:

Agents come in all shapes and sizes. Some offer their services to simply help a sponsor (librarian in this case) locate the author/speaker that is being sought out; but others have "stables" of speakers whom they (the agent) represent exclusively. In this latter case, librarians should always go to the agent, as even if they approach the publisher, the librarians will often be sent back to the agent. I suppose there's no harm in asking a publisher, so maybe one should always try, but after trial and error, and time on the job, it will become fairly evident the agents and publicists one can develop a relationship with. Because librarians already have full-time jobs, it can be confusing navigating the world of agents and publicists. I think it is important to know one's budget, to stick by your "figures" and remember the mission at hand: most likely this would be to create public programs with authors in a way that stimulates the local cultural landscape. It is good and important work. On the other hand, it's always good to remember that the author being invited will have heard from dozens of other librarians before, so do not simply rely on the author's sense of altruism, as they may already have a long list of such causes before yours. This realization would not diminish your cause, but only help you see more accurately both sides.

I would also say that it is important to talk to your colleagues; ask them which agents have been helpful, or which ones have not. Which agents have gone the extra mile to really represent the interest of the library (in this case) and not just the author? I think a frequent exchange with colleagues around the country helps gather information before a call is made to an agent. If you find that the ALA or PLA lacks the resources of names and numbers of other libraries presenting talks or readings, then resort to good old detective work online by simply entering "library" and "lecture" in any major search engine online. This will also help you see what your colleagues are doing.

I can hear you thinking, "How much does it cost to hire an author through an agent?" Like anything, it depends on the appeal of the author and the demand for his time. My experience has been that $3,000 is a rock-bottom price and this will be for a little-known author, $5,000 will get you someone a little better known and $10,000 may get someone you've actually heard of. These fees are in addition to lodging and transportation costs. The quote that will stick forever in my head was for a well-known but not wildly famous broadcaster/author who required a $70,000 fee plus transportation via private jet. And this was several years ago. I suppose this isn't much in the rarified climes celebrities inhabit, but at the public agency level, it's nothing less than astonishing.

Authors who don't want to be bothered with appearances adjust their fees accordingly. You can't blame them really. An author who has received some fame may find herself drowning in requests for personal appearances when what she really wants is some time to write. I've heard more than one children's author lament that although winning the American Library Association's prestigious Newbery Award was a rare honor, it also took them away from writing for a year or two while they fulfilled all the publicity requests that resulted. But I digress ...

I've dealt with agents who are fabulous and agents who are heinous; it's the luck of the draw. As Steven suggests, do as much research as you can. It is helpful to talk to other folks who have had dealings with agents. Some authors are actually listed with more than one agency, interestingly enough.

It's helpful to remember that when you enter the world of speaker's bureaus, you've entered the world of sales. An agent's goal may often be to get you a speaker from his agency's stable for your gig. If he can get you the one you wanted, that's fine, but it's not necessarily his first priority. Rarely will you get a direct answer to a question such as, "How much does Stephen King cost?" You'll be mined for information about your event, your budget, your audience so that the agent can suggest another author from his agency if need be. As Steven noted, some agents are able to do this with true empathy for your needs; some are not.

Once you make yourself known to an agency, you are on its list. Someone from the agency will check in with you on a regular basis to ascertain your needs. Hey, it's an honest buck. It's just easier to deal with if you know it's coming—especially if you normally live in the relatively protected world of nonprofits or public agencies.

Should you choose to work with a speaker's bureau, here's a list of contact information. If you spend some time surfing through the various Web sites, you'll get an inkling of the kind of speakers each agency represents.

Speakers' Agents

American Program Bureau
36 Crafts Street
Newton, MA 02458
800.225.4575
Fax: (617) 965.6610
http://www.apbspeakers.com
E-mail: apb@apbspeakers.com

Authors Unlimited
31 East 32nd Street
Suite 300
New York, NY 10016
(212) 481.8484
Fax: (212) 481.9582
http://www.authorsunlimited.com
E-mail: contact@authorsunlimited.com

Greater Talent Network, Inc.
150 Fifth Avenue
New York, NY 10011
(212) 645.4200
Fax: (212) 627.1471
http://www.greatertalent.com
E-mail: info@greatertalent.com

Jodi F. Solomon Speakers Bureau
325 Huntington Avenue Suite 112
Boston, MA 02115
(617) 266.3450
Fax: (617) 266.5660
http://www.jodisolomonspeakers.com
E-mail: jodi@jodisolomon.biz

Keppler Associates Inc.
4350 North Fairfax Drive, Suite 700
Arlington, VA 22203
(703) 516.4000
Fax: (703) 516.4819
http://www.kepplerspeakers.com

Royce Carlton, Incorporated
866 United Nations Plaza
Suite 587
New York, NY 10017-1880
(212) 355.7700
(800) L-E-C-T-U-R-E (toll free)
Fax: (212) 888.8659
http://www.roycecarlton.com
E-mail: info@roycecarlton.com

Speakers Worldwide, Inc.
PO Box 30195
Bethesda, MD 20814
(301) 365.1010
(800) 408.7757 (toll free)
Fax: (301) 767.9787
http://www.speakersworldwide.com
E-mail: spkrsww@aol.com

ICM Beverly Hills
8942 Wilshire Boulevard
Beverly Hills, CA 90211
(310) 550.4000
http://icmtalent.com
E-mail: books@icmtalent.com

International Creative Management
ICM New York
40 West 57th Street
New York, NY 10019
(212) 556.5600
Fax: (212) 556.5647

Steven Barclay Agency
321 Pleasant Street
Petaluma, CA 94952
(707) 773.0654
(888) 965.7323 (toll free)
Fax: 707.778.1868
http://www.barclayagency.com
E-mail: steven@barclayagency.com

Working with Cultural Clearinghouses

You may have access to other arts organizations that will help you find, fund and promote author events. For instance, the mission of the American Library Association's Public Programs Office is to help libraries create quality cultural programming as an integral part of library service. This includes author events. Their "Live at the Library" has showcased many authors and poets for librarians at conferences and helped librarians bring authors home. You can look at the variety of programs available to you on www.ala.org.

Do a little research and you may find other state or national organizations that will support an author event. The Des Moines Public Library enlisted Humanities Iowa as a sponsor for AViD (Authors Visiting in Des Moines). The National Endowment for the Arts (www.nea.gov) has begun funding The Big Read to encourage communities to come together to read and discuss one book. These sorts of programs might not have funding for the specific author you have in mind, but you can see how their programs fit into your goals.

Don't forget about poets when you're thinking about authors. Poets House works to make connections between libraries and poets through its national Poetry in the Branches. The folks at Poets House believe that "live experiences with engaging poets can create a lasting connection between readers and poetry." To this end they train librarians to design and present an event and connect them with poets who can reach their patrons. For more information, check out their Web site, www.poetshouse.org.

So it's your choice how to track down and book an author. Bear in mind that not every author is available to do speaking engagements. Some accept engagements solely through their agents. Some don't do book tours. And some do but are perfectly awful at it. Do a little investigation before you commit to an author. You can ask the publisher, respectfully, how comfortable a particular author is in front of an audience. Editors and publicists will often be candid with you. It's in their best interests to feature a writer's strengths, and if speaking isn't one of them, well, so be it. You can also make inquiries online on a listserv such as Fiction-L. (I've included subscription information in the Additional Resources section.) Ask for personal responses, though, so you're not in the position of gossiping to a national audience.

It's also worthwhile to keep your ears open for hints of authors who are high maintenance. Does she need her Perrier placed just so on the podium? Will you be expected to be a dog sitter for the precious ones? It's nice to know in advance what foibles you'll be dealing with, if you can. That way you can decide how far down that road you want to go.

Volunteer Authors

I'll always remember the first time I heard the word "volunteer" applied to plants. It tickled me to call a posy that just popped up a volunteer. Sometime volunteer authors are terrific, sometimes not so much—just like those California poppies in my yard.

The opposite end of the spectrum from seeking out popular authors is dealing with little-known authors who want an author event at the library. I'd bet that nearly anyone who has done programming for a library has encountered this situation. Big Jim Jones, who has coached Little League baseball for thirty years, has put together and self-published a book on baseball. Jim calls to see if the library would like to sponsor an author event. Well … maybe.

I applaud these authors who are trying like crazy to market their books. Unfortunately, an author event at the library is rarely the answer for you or for them. David Domkoski, Public Relations Director for Tacoma Public Library, reckons that events for first novelists are the most challenging programs to do. Those are the cases when twenty people can be counted a huge success. And these are first novelists who have the weight of a major publishing house behind them. Events for first novelists who are self-published are even more difficult, if not impossible, to pull off.

Unless the topic happens to be especially interesting or provocative or there are other connections that tie in with your criteria for doing author events, it's difficult to make this kind of event fly. Deborah A. Robertson in *Cultural Programming for Libraries* suggests keeping an open mind about unpublished and self-published authors, asking to see the material and then making a judgment on a case-by-case basis. Judy Butler says her criteria is pretty clear: "I tell local authors that we only do events for celebrities or those who are on the *New York Times* Bestseller List. When they tell me they're *going* to be on the *New York Times* Bestseller List, I reply that I'll kick myself when that day comes and regret that lost opportunity."

Another program planner throws an open house for new authors once a year just so they have a forum. The audience mostly consists of the authors and their families, but everyone seems to have a good time.

King County Library System solved the problem at one point by hosting a virtual open house for any interested local authors on their Web site. "In Their Own Words" featured a brief audio recording of the author talking about his or her book along with a photo of the author and the book cover graphic.

Deborah Schneider, who is in the unique position of being a programmer and an author, cautions against being too softhearted. "Every author who wants to have a library event has to present a pretty compelling case to me. There is no such thing as a 'free' program even if there is no charge. Making the arrangements, sending out publicity, even setting up the room costs staff time. Staff time is money. We have to be judicious in the use of that resource."

So there's no easy answer for "volunteer authors." Much as you hate to discourage a budding writer, you have to judge what you think the return for your institution is compared with the outlay of time and effort. And if you're an author who wants to volunteer, check in Chapter 14 for tips on how to do it.

5

Query Letters and Proposals

If you've seen the musical *Gypsy*, you know that novice stripper Gypsy Rose Lee receives advice from the more seasoned performers in the musical number "You Gotta Have a Gimmick." Well, maybe you don't *gotta* have a gimmick for an author event, but the one thing I hear over and over again from authors and publicists is that they love events that have an imaginative twist and aren't just the same old speech followed by a question-and-answer session. I'm very impressed by such events myself and often lament my own lack of imagination. Once, desperate to respond in kind to a publisher who wanted something unique for a Jean Auel appearance, I suggested a concurrent display of ancient Aleut artifacts from the Natural History Museum accompanied by Native American drummers. Jean Auel went elsewhere. Ah, well.

There are others, fortunately, who can really work an angle. Here's one that really took the cake.

When I asked an author of hardboiled mysteries what his best author appearance experience was, he shuddered expressively and replied, "There isn't any such thing!" Then upon reflection he told me this story:

> When my first book came out I had a friend who worked at Nordstrom in the cosmetics department. She offered to do a book event for me in the store. I was very, very doubtful but I eventually agreed. The event was called, get this, "Don't Let Your Skin Be a Mystery." They plunked me down, honest to God, in the middle of the cosmetics department with skin care demonstrations and who knows what all going on around me. It was a mob scene. I sold every book. Then they sent two salesgirls out to every bookstore in the mall to buy out their stock of my book. I sold every one of those books. My agent had come because he was sure I'd need consolation, and he was astounded. It was the best author event I've ever had. Not only that, I dated off the phone numbers I got that night for two years. And so did my agent. "Don't Let Your Skin Be a Mystery," for crying out loud.

It occurs to me that maybe not every author would thrive on this kind of event, but it certainly worked in this case.

While I'm not the most creative type on the block, I do have a couple of tricks that have worked pretty well for attracting an author (and an audience) to a program.

The Series

Authors in a series seem to work well for us. It makes the individual author appearance part of something bigger, and it gives you a chance to cultivate an ever-larger audience as you go along. At our library, we've declared this year to be the year of the mystery. As part of "Make Mine a Mystery," we're hosting authors Ridley Pearson, Laura Lippman, Jacqueline Winspear and J. A. Jance. Because the Pacific Northwest seems to be hotbed of mystery writers, we might offer a panel discussion of fun but lesser-known local mystery writers like the charming Curt Colbert or Mary Daheim. Skye Kathleen Moody and G. M. Ford, mystery writers and husband and wife, is in the works. The point is to build momentum and keep your theme rolling throughout the year. It's interesting to note that Poet's House recommends a minimum of three events for those planning poetry programming so that you have a chance to build an audience.

The Conversation

One year I had a brilliant idea (I thought) and designed on ongoing program in which I interviewed a series of authors. We conjured up a raised platform and a couple of overstuffed chairs. We put a small table between the chairs (for water and coffee, don't you know?), and placed a big plant artfully in the background. Homey, yes?

I have to say I sweated bullets before each event. I do not have a degree in literature; I'm just a reader and librarian. I've talked to plenty of people, but I'm not a journalist either. I swallowed hard, did my homework, read each book carefully and prepared questions that I wanted to know, that I thought the majority of the audience wanted to know or that would let the author expand on the book in an interesting way. I'm glad to report it worked wonderfully. Some authors, like Jacqueline Mitchard or Erik Larson, could hold forth engagingly with no assistance from me, but they graciously pretended that I was having an impact on the proceedings. Other authors, like Bharti Kirchner and Harriet Scott Chessman, became very comfortable chatting away with me and really bloomed in the interview process.

One of the interesting things that happened is that the audience became engaged and involved in the conversation to a greater degree than normal. They would often ask impromptu questions as we were chatting along, sometimes to a point where I was feeling a little superfluous. It changed from a passive event to an interactive one. I don't know if it was the homey atmosphere or the conversational format, but it turned out to be great fun for the audience, the authors and me.

The Panel

As I mentioned earlier, I really like the idea of a panel of authors. It lets you develop a theme and has the potential of bringing in a bigger audience than one author alone might draw. Plus, the authors have more fun. Judi Snyder, who runs "Bookmania!" for Martin County Library in Florida, loves author panels. "Unless I have a major headliner, and maybe even if I do, I love to pack four or five authors together in a panel. Audience members may each come for a different author, but in the end I'm broadening readers' choice of books."

Ain't No Town Like Our Town

One of the things I learned in chatting with other library folk about author events is that you can use your own hometown as a selling point when you are asking an author to come. One woman volunteered that her small Alaska town was fabulously scenic and had an equally fabulous and famous bed and breakfast to entice authors to come. Another declared that the terrific fishing in her area catapulted her town to a strategic stop for authors on tour. If you do a little investigation, you might find other attractions as well, and not always the physical variety. One event planner discovered that the author she was pining after had family in the area. When a family wedding came up, so did the opportunity for an author event.

My favorite story is one that Judy (remember Judy from Utah?) shared with me. Judy was determined to bring Charles Osgood to her small Utah town. Judy kept her eyes and ears open and built an ever-expanding dossier on her quest. Upon learning that Mr. Osgood was a music lover, Judy took her shot. She contacted the director of the Mormon Tabernacle Choir and asked if they would consider Mr. Osgood as a guest artist. Indeed they would, Judy learned. Armed with that information Judy made her proposal to Mr. Osgood, adding that a guest appearance with the Mormon Tablernacle Choir could be arranged in conjunction with his appearance at her library. Talk about capturing someone's attention. And it all came to pass. Charles Osgood spoke at Judy's library, played the piano with the choir and proved himself to be one of the most kindly and gracious men on the planet. Is there a happier ending?

The Proposal

You may approach authors or publishers in any way that's comfortable to you. Here are some samples of how it might be done. Judy's advice is to remember the secretaries and assistants who work with your author, especially if the authors are famous folk. Judy spent as much time and energy chatting with Charles Osgood's secretary as she did with the great man himself, and it was the secretary who conveniently reminded him when the time was right.

Judy is a huge fan of the phone. As a matter of fact, she doesn't have an e-mail account. She doesn't want anyone to be able to turn her down until she's actually talked to him or her. Judy is a great talker, and her success rate is phenomenal.

I don't hold a candle to Judy in the talking department. I really like e-mail. It's convenient for both the recipient and me. This is especially true when you take different time zones into account. My library is three hours behind New York. That makes the window of opportunity for a phone call very small and specific. The other great thing about e-mail is that I can make sure my thoughts are composed.

Even if authors are on the road, they'll check in with their e-mail. I think e-mail has become a very standard way of doing business. Yes, it's easy to ignore as well, but I figure I can always talk as a second line of offense. Here's an e-mail that I shot off to a well-known local author last week. I got the address from her Web page.

To: Susan Wiggs   **From:** Chapple Langemack

RE: Program at the Bellevue Regional Library

Hi Susan,

I'm the Managing Librarian at the Bellevue Regional Library. We'd love to host you for an author event here in June 2006. Would that be a possibility? We can certainly offer transportation expenses and an honorarium. Thanks for considering it.

Chapple Langemack

I got a gracious acceptance before the end of the day.

This e-mail invitation offers a little more information and took an unconventional approach:

To: Scott Simon   **From:** Chapple Langemack

Subject: Speaking Engagement in Seattle

Hi Scott,

It can't be every day that you get propositioned by a public library.

I'm writing on behalf of the King County Library System Foundation to invite you to be the keynote speaker at our "Literary Lions" banquet in Bellevue, Washington next March.

King County Library System surrounds the city of Seattle and serves about a million folks with libraries. The KCLS Foundation is our nonprofit/development arm. The "Literary Lions" banquet is the annual really big do—dinner after hours in our largest library for about 350 people. Thirty or so local authors are also invited and everybody gets the chance to meet and greet and get books signed.

The great thing is that the keynote speech is pretty short—20 to 30 minutes, and you can say what you like. While we always love to hear how fabulous libraries are, we'd be just as happy to hear about you. We would, of course, pay your travel and lodging expenses as well as an honorarium. We're trying for the first or second Saturday in March, but at this point we are somewhat flexible.

Please let me know what it would take to entice you to come and hang out with some pretty cool library folk for an evening. (I know, I know, I'm terribly biased.) We'd be so glad to have you come.

Thanks for considering the invitation.

Chapple Langemack
Readers' Services Coordinator
King County Library System

Sometimes, all you're able to come up with is a mailing address. Then it's time for a brief, pleasant letter. Think of this as you would a cover letter for your resume. All you need to do is intrigue the author enough for her to make contact. She doesn't need chapter and verse at this point. Here's one that Claire shoots off, also for the Literary Lions event and a little more subdued.

Dear Mr. Atkinson,

On behalf of the King County Library System Foundation, I would like to invite you and your guest to be our guests at the Literary Lions Gala on Saturday, March 11, 2006, at the Bellevue Regional Library. This event features thirty Northwest authors and books by those authors at a benefit book sale before our fundraising dinner. I've attached a fact sheet to give you an overview of the event.

We would be delighted if you could join us! Please let me know by January 2, if possible, so that I can include your name on our list of authors in the formal invitation to our donors and supporters. I hope we can look forward to enjoying your company.

Claire Wilkinson
Development Specialist
King County Library System Foundation

Claire includes a fact sheet with more information. I've included the fact sheet in the appendix if you want to take a look.

If you are working with a publisher, you'll want to submit a more formal proposal. Here's where you put all those details from Chapter 2 that you thought so hard and long about. Here's a sample guide that one of the publishers gave me:

Library Author Appearance Request

Name of Library: Address of Library:

Library Programming Contact:

Event Name:

Series Name (if event is part of a series):

Frequency of events in this series:

Is event cosponsored by Friends, Foundation, Local Newspaper or Business? Explain.

Event Date(s):   Event Time: Event Format:

Meal Function? Breakfast/Luncheon/Dinner/etc.:

Reading/Lecture/Talk/Panel Discussion:

Q&A:

Number of authors speaking:

     If other authors are confirmed, please list:

Length of each author's presentation:

Audience makeup:

Anticipated audience size:

Book selling:

To follow event?

On-site?

Who sells books: Library/Friends of the Library/local bookstore:

     If local bookstore, please name:

Do you handle book sales prior to the event?

     If so, how?

Publicity:

Prior to event:

flyers/posters/bookmarks/newsletters/pressreleases/newspaper/magazine/radio/television

At the event:

newspaper/radio/television/etc.

After the event:

newsletters/newpaper/magazine/radio/television

Please name specific media outlets for each scenario

Past authors at this event:

Past authors at this library:

Expenses:

Will the library provide money for hotel/airfare/car service/meals

Will the library provide an honorarium:

If so, please state the honorarium:

Comments/Special Notes:

Please include any notes or details about this event that would make it particularly special (i.e., Does the author have a connection with your library/town? Does the book take place in your town? is there a special theme for this event? Is there a relevant art exhibit/performance that would tie in with this book/author?) Pleas don't hesitate to be creative—but please let us know if these plans are tentative or confirmed.

From *Author Event Primer: How to Plan, Execute and Enjoy Author Events* by Chapple Langemack. Westport, CT: Libraries Unlimited. Copyright © 2007 by Chapple Langemack.

Here's a sample of a submitted request. Michael Harkovitch (then a programming intern, now a sterling reference librarian) put this one together.

Library Author Appearance Request: Dave Barry

King County Library System, 960 Newport Way NW, Issaquah, WA 98027
Library Programming Contact: Chapple Langemack, (425) 369-3318
E-mail: chaplang@kcls.org

We'd like to feature Dave Barry in one of our author events. The venue would be the gorgeous 402-seat Kirkland Performance Center, and the event would be cosponsored by King County Library System, Park Place Books and the Kirkland Performance Center.

Event name: An evening with Dave Barry

Event Dates: Whenever author and venue are mutually available.

Event Time: Prefer evening – 7:30 P.M.

Event Format: Remarks/Reading, followed by Q&A.

Audience makeup: Adults and teens from throughout the greater Seattle area.

Anticipated audience size: 400. We anticipate this event to be very popular.

Book selling: Sales before and after the program on site by Park Place Books.

Publicity prior to event: 8,000 brochures distributed through 42 community library sites, posters, flyers and e-mail notification to our "author alert" list of 800 people who have asked to be notified of upcoming author visits. We would also include it in a newsletter that goes out to 6,000 adults participating in our "Reading Rewards" program. New releases will be sent to all newspapers in the area, and radio and television stations will be contacted. This author appearance will be featured on our Web site (http://www.kcls.org), which receives more than 9 million hits per month.

Publicity at the Event: It would be expected that the *Seattle Times, The Seattle Post-Intelligencer, The Eastside Journal, The Seattle Weekly* and representatives from other media would attend.

Past Authors at KCLS events: Tom Robbins, Robert Hass, Malachy McCourt, Joyce Carol Oates, Rick Bragg, Jacquelyn Mitchard, Nikki Giovanni, Mark Salzman, Molly Gloss, Ha Jin, David James Duncan, Lisa Scottoline, Susan Isaacs, David Rakoff, Mary Higgins Clark, Laurie R. King, Elizabeth George, Robert Pinsky and Adriana Trigiani have all spoken at the King County Library System.

Expenses: Library staff can assist with ground transportation .

Comments: Dave Barry's books circulate heavily at KCLS. An author event featuring Mr. Barry will be very popular among our service population.

Here's a slightly different proposal written by Deborah Schneider. Debbie felt she needed to give additional background on the library system. She loved it when the publicist found her effort "impressive":

Proposal for Hosting Author Event: James Patterson

From: Deborah Schneider, Public Programming Coordinator
King County Library System, 960 Newport Way NW, Issaquah, WA 98027
(425) 369.3319; E-mail: dschneider@kcls.org

The King County Library System (KCLS) is one of the largest circulating libraries in the United States. The Library System includes forty-three libraries located in the communities surrounding Seattle, Washington, a Traveling Library Center, a Techlab and five library institutions. Nearly 1.3 million residents utilize the vast resources of KCLS, with more than 19 million items having been checked out in 2005. The KCLS Web site (www.kcls.org) receives an average of 9 million hits per month.

KCLS offers a collection of 4 million items, with books, periodicals, newspapers and pamphlets, audio and videotapes, films, compact discs, DVDs, MP3 Players (eAudio), books on cassette, downloadable e-books and extensive online resources and databases. Materials are available system-wide and can be requested and sent to any local library within the system.

For more information about the King County Library System, visit our Web site at: www.kcls.org. Successful events have included the following authors:

Terry Brooks, Jayne Ann Krentz, Phillipa Gregory, Joanne Harris, Karen Cushman, J.A. Jance, Debbie Macomber, John Nance, Sherman Alexie, Malachy McCourt, Tom Robbins, Mercedes Lackey, Jennifer Crusie, Gordon Korman, Gary Paulsen, Jack Prelutsky, Deb Caletti and Darren Shan.

Since 2001 we have hosted an annual lecture series for Young Adults called "The Kim Lafferty Memorial Lectures," named for one of our employees who had a huge impact on the way the King County Library System regards young adult books. The authors for this series have included Chris Crutcher, Will Hobbs, Tamora Pierce, Jack Gantos and Gordon Korman. These lectures are offered at a performing arts center, and local schools bus their students to the site. In the evening a public program is held at one of our larger libraries. We have had audiences of up to 1,200 students for this event.

Throughout the year we work with schools, taking a wide range of programs including authors to school audiences. We are very proud of the partnerships we have developed and successful events we've offered.

Author Event Request

Dates: May 22–June 9, 2006 (would prefer week of May 22–26)

Event: The daytime event would be held at Skyline High School, 1122 228th Avenue SE, Sammamish, WA 98075

The school theater will hold 409 students, and students from two surrounding junior high schools would also be invited. Program to be approximately one hour in length.

Evening Program: Because we feel this would attract a very large audience, we would work with one of the Performing Arts Centers we have an arrangement with to seat as many people as possible. Program to be approximately one hour in length and followed by book signing.

Estimated Audience Size: 350–500

Local Media Coverage: A recent author event included an interview with KOMO 1000 radio, news releases, a local newspaper interview, a follow-up interview with *The Seattle Times* and a crew from *Evening Magazine,* a local news magazine show filming for the entire two-hour event for broadcast in February. We have a community relations office that works on publicity and press releases to the media. We have an e-mail reminder system that notifies subscribers of author events.

Book Sales and Signing: We have ongoing relationships with many bookstores, including All For Kids, University Book Store and Kim Ricketts, Independent Bookseller. Books are available for sale at all of our author events.

Thank you for offering the King County Library System this opportunity.

Deborah Schneider, Public Programming Coordinator

You don't always need a full-blown, bells and whistles proposal. Here's a more informal proposal that I submitted to a publisher's representative whom I'd worked with many times:

To: Lucy Publisher   **From:** Chapple Langemack

RE: Lisa Scottoline at King County Library System

Hi Lucy,

We'd love to include Lisa Scottoline in our "Authors in Conversation" program at the Bellevue Regional Library. This series features authors chatting with King County Library System's Readers' Services Coordinator, Chapple Langemack in a relaxed and personal forum that is more intimate and more engaging than a standard author lecture or reading. Other authors confirmed for this series in 2003 include Jacquelyn Mitchard, Erik Larson and Harriet Scott Chessman. A June event featuring Lisa would be perfect. We would expect an audience of 200 people.

Publicity would include 8,000 brochures distributed through 43 community library sites, posters, flyers and e-mail notification to our "author alert" list of 6,000 people who have asked to be notified of upcoming author visits. This author appearance will be featured on our Web site (www.kcls.org), which receives more than 9 million hits per month. We will also have some money to devote to paid advertising for this event.

The University Book Store will cosponsor this series, managing sales at the author programs and lending their considerable weight to publicizing the events.

Thanks, Lucy. I look forward to hearing from you.

Chapple

I know it sounds weird to refer to myself in the third person, but realize she's going to send this on to others. It's helpful if she doesn't have to re-write it.

If you've done author events in the past, it's helpful to have a track re-cord, but it's not absolutely necessary. Everyone starts somewhere. Just have a good plan in mind and give it your best effort.

You really only need these kinds of queries and proposals when you're dealing directly with an author or a publisher. If you are working with an agent, communication is much more cut and dried. However, you still need to know the basics of audience, location, budget and the like. Just call or shoot off an e-mail asking for your desired author and date. I guarantee you'll get an immediate response from the agent either with what's required for the author you want or with queries about your purpose and budget so they can match you with another speaker.

When I asked Judy Butler for the best advice she could give program planners, especially those without much money, she said, "Don't be afraid to ask! Be pleasant, be persistent, but ask. All they can do is say no." Now you know how to ask, get out there and get to asking.

6

Getting Down to Business

Once you've gotten an agreement for an author to come to do a program for you, it's time to put it in writing. Whether you are dealing directly with the author, with the publisher or with an agent, you need to clearly lay out the expectations and the finances. If you are dealing directly with the author, it can be fairly simple. If you are dealing with a publisher, there will be more people to keep in the loop. If you are dealing with an agent, then the paperwork will be pretty straightforward, but you still have to pay close attention to your own best interests.

Setting a Fee

This seems to be the hardest thing for us nonprofit folks to deal with. How much money do we offer? How little can we get away with? The good news is that as you do this over time, you'll get some feeling for the going rate. I always wanted to offer my local authors a reasonable sum for their time. It may not have been a fortune, but I figured part of the library's job was to support our local authors. $200–$300 seemed appropriate. Not a fortune, perhaps, but an expression of our appreciation. Perhaps it's $50–$100 in your community. This is just something you have to play by ear and experiment with. Remember that in many cases the author doesn't know what a fee should be either. One of the parameters you can think about while you'll mulling over what fee to offer is the size of the audience you expect to have. If you expect 200 people, what "per head" cost are you willing to incur? If publicity for your agency is what you're after, you may do your accounting a little differently to take into consideration what the attention paid to this event is buying for you.

My favorite recollection of striking an agreement with an author is when I was negotiating with a well-known mystery author who had agreed to come to Seattle to do an event for our "Women of Mystery" series. Lovely and gracious, she wouldn't say what an appropriate honorarium would be. I made an offer, probably a little high because I love her books so much. She replied, "Well, you can give me that much, but I'd just have to donate it to the Friends of the Library." We settled on a lower figure. Now I not only love her books, I love her.

More than likely, what you offer will depend on what you have. As my friend Omar would say, "And now we go to the marketplace. How much money do you have in your pocket?" If you have no money if your pocket, it still may be possible to snag an author. Book tours are your best bet in that case. You have to plan well, be pleasant, be persistent and be flexible.

Judy started her hugely successful author programming with no money at all. She says you have to point out all of the positives about your event and your venue and hope for the best.

Whether there is money on the table or not, don't take it personally if an author declines. And don't be afraid to ask again later (remember that pleasant persistence). We recently hosted a local mystery author who still works at his day job full time even though he has more than a dozen novels published. This is a gentleman whose time is dear. He had declined invitations several times, but this time, the stars were in alignment, and he came, much to the audience's delight. He mentioned that he had been asked to another event several years in a row and he'd had to say no. He said he was feeling so guilty about it that he'd probably accept the next invitation. I sincerely hope those folks ask again.

Remember too when you're settling a deal to clarify expectations about when the author will be paid. Will you mail a check in advance of the event? Will the check come after the event? Or will you slip them an envelope during the course of the event itself?

My own experience as a speaker has been that I absorb all the upfront expenses, like plane fare and hotel rooms, myself and then submit my receipts and am reimbursed, sometimes more promptly, sometimes not so promptly. Although I totally understand the reasoning behind this technique, I can't say that this is an ideal situation from the speaker's point of view. You are often left with that plane fare burning a hole in your credit card for a couple of months in advance of the event. I do prefer making my own travel arrangements, however, so the alternative of the event planners making the arrangements isn't appealing either. I guess the moral to this story is that you should take this kind of situation into consideration when making an offer for an honorarium. Or there is Plan B, which is what we use.

The Inclusive Fee

When we first began hosting authors, we set up an account at a local hotel. The author's stay would be billed directly to the library. Most meals were purchased by the author's staff escort and reimbursed. That got problematic because staff members are not able to be reimbursed for their own meals. And if the author wanted to live it up after the event and go drinking with you at the top of the Space Needle, well, you could just kiss your mortgage payment goodbye. Then there was the issue of the hotel bill. Paying for lodging was fine. But our auditor took a dim view of the library paying for a guest's phone bills, dry cleaning and bar bills. Clearly it was time for a different tactic.

Now we make a lump sum offer. We make an educated guess about how much travel, food and lodging will cost from the author's home. Then we add in the honorarium. Then we make the inclusive offer. That way if the author wants to camp out, fine. If he wants to put the money toward staying at the Ritz, fabulous. And we neither know nor care about his cleaning, drinking and communication habits. And the best part is that the auditor is happy. The payment is a fee for an author event. Period.

This is an arrangement you can make through an agent, but it's not the way agents are accustomed to doing business so you have to be clear, clear and clear again. Read the contract carefully and make sure it is an accurate representation of what you intend.

Setting Expectations

Money isn't the only thing you need to clarify in writing when you're hammering out terms. You need to specify very clearly what it is you expect the author to do. Do you expect the author to visit a school? How many classes? For how long? What else are they expected to do that day? It need not always be complicated, but it does need to be clear. Here's a sample.

26 April 2006
Mr. Edgar Allen Poe
3382 Raven Drive
Baltimore, MD 30044

Dear Mr. Poe:

I'm so pleased that you will be able to participate in "Voices from the Edge," King County Library System's fall author series. This letter outlines our expectations regarding your presentation. Please review this agreement. If you have no questions, please complete and sign the enclosed contract and then return it to me in the envelope provided.

You will be making the following presentations:

- 45-minute speech/reading at the Issaquah Library (10 Sunset Way, Issaquah, WA 98027)

  Followed by a 15-minute Q&A session and book signing on 18 September 2001 from 3:30–5 P.M.

  An independent bookseller will be present for book sales.

  This will be a relatively informal presentation at one of our larger community libraries. It's always hard to anticipate attendance, but we would expect 75–100 people.

- 45-minute speech/reading at the Kirkland Performance Center (350 Kirkland Avenue, Kirkland, WA 98033)

  Followed by a 15-minute Q&A session and book signing on 18 September 2001 from 7:30–9 P.M.

  An independent bookseller will be present for book sales.

  This venue is a lovely 400-seat theatre and feels more formal. It is right next door to our Kirkland Library, and it's possible that the book signing will take place at the library.

King County Library System will pay you $X,XXX, which is inclusive of honorarium and all fees and expenses with the understanding that these are exclusive appearances in the Seattle area. We appreciate your not participating in book signings or other events at other venues while you are here under contract to King County Library System. You will receive your check within one week of the event.

A King County Library System staff member will meet you at the airport and take you to your hotel and from your hotel to all appearances. The Woodmark Hotel in Kirkland is just minutes away from the evening venue, and many of our authors have chosen to stay there. Their internet address is http://www.thewoodmark.com/ should you wish to investigate.

Thank you for being a part of this exciting series. Our patrons are a warm and enthusiastic audience. We are all looking forward to your visit. Should you have questions, please contact me at 425.369.3318 or via e-mail at chaplang@kcls.org.

Cordially,

Chapple Langemack
Reader's Services Coordinator

When you're getting an author through a publisher, the letter of expectations often comes from the publicist. Here's a sample:

Dear Chapple:

This letter confirms your event with Rick Bragg, author of Ava's Man, for Saturday, September 28, 2002.

Rick Bragg will arrive at 1:45 P.M. for a reading and signing from 2:00 P.M. to 3:00 P.M. at the KING COUNTY LIBRARY located at 960 Newport Way NW.

A press kit and jacket blow-up will follow this confirmation to help you in promoting the event (if requested, additional materials such as extra photos and jackets are always available to you). If you have any special contacts with local media, please let me know so that I can send materials right away.

Best,

Jane Doe

Publicists are great. Like Jane mentioned, they'll often send you posters, bookmarks and other goodies to help you promote the event. Don't forget the publisher's library marketing person, though. Make sure you keep her in the loop. Copy her on your e-mails to the publicist and check in by phone from time to time. You'll gain two things by this: no one will be duplicating efforts because everyone will know what's going on and the more the library marketing person knows about your track record with authors, the more she'll be able to pitch for you with other publicists.

I saved this confirmation e-mail for a speaking engagement I once did because it made everything so clear:

To: Chapple   **From:** Mary

RE: Speaking Engagement at BIGCO

Dear Chapple,

Thank your for agreeing to come and speak with our employees on nonfiction and memoirs representing diversity. Per our conversation you will be doing a total of four presentations.

Here are the details:

Location: BIGCO Home Office, February 25, 2006
   King Auditorium, 2nd Floor Mezzanine
   Time: First Presentation—11:00 A.M. to 11:45 A.M.
   Second Presentation—12:00 P.M. to 12:45 P.M.

Directions: From I-5 North take exit 169 (NE 45th). Keep right at the fork in the ramp. Turn right onto 12th Avenue NE. The parking garage is on the right. Please park in the visitors' parking lot.

Host: Barney Thunem, Diversity Planning Committee

Location: BIGCO Redmond Campus, February 27, 2006
   Rainier King Auditorium, Rainier Building
   Time: Third Presentation—11:00 A.M. to 11:45 A.M.
   Fourth Presentation—12:00 P.M. to 12:45 P.M.

Directions: From I-5 North take exit 168B (Highway 520 East). Take the NE 51st Street exit and turn right. Take your first right into the BIGCO Redmond Campus at NE 154th Avenue NE. Please park in the North garage located on the left or adjacent to the Rainier building.

Host: Chris Larsen, Diversity Planning Committee

I will be sending you further information when we are closer to the program. Thanks again for agreeing to come and speak with us.

If you're dealing with an agent, the paperwork, the expectations and the timing of the check will all follow a standard format. Your challenge here will be to insert any needs you have that are out of the ordinary—like the inclusive payment. You can do it if you know what you need and are prepared.

The expectations part of the process is where you learn, or should learn, what the author's expectations are. When you're dealing with an agent, this will be clearly spelled out in the contract, sometimes down to the kind of car they will or will not ride in. I heard a rumor that every dressing room of every venue in which Barry Manilow performs must be painted a particular shade of champagne pink. Luckily I haven't run into anything like that yet.

Publicists will give you a heads up as to an author's druthers as well. One that particularly tickled me was when we hosted Tom Robbins. Tom lives in the Northwest and has a near cult following. We filled a 400-seat house with folks thrilled to death to be able to see and hear him. Of course, many of them had been drinking Coronas in the parking lot for quite a while before the event, so they had even more cause to be happy. The publicist for Tom's publisher let me know that Tom liked to have a snack after he spoke, while he was signing books. What kind of snack, I queried. The publicist was a little vague, "Oh, cookies, maybe." My colleagues and I mulled this over with a seriousness akin to Geneva Convention deliberations. What constituted a proper snack for Tom Robbins? If cookies, what kind? How about fruit? Cheese, maybe? In the end I think we opted for a little bit of everything. I'm not sure there was room on the table to sign books for the snack-laden tray.

One matter that can be a point of contention is when the author actually arrives in town. If he or she is on a book tour, you may not have any influence in the matter at all. If it's at all possible, however, it's terrific when the author can come in the day before the event. Rest and refreshment aside, airline schedules aren't what they used to be, and if an author misses a flight or if a flight is cancelled for some reason, there may not be another very soon. Or at least soon enough to save your event from being toast (and I don't mean a snack).

A Lesson I Learned the Hard Way

Here's a story from our own experience.

One of the things I didn't think about when I first started doing author events was an exclusivity agreement. I didn't even think to think about it. I just made the arrangements assuming the author would come and go home again. Then we hosted one particular well-known and prolific author. We paid her a handsome sum to keynote at a fundraising dinner one night and then do a public event the next evening. Imagine my surprise when I picked her up for the second event and found that she had been visiting bookstores all day. She'd been doing "drive bys"—going to a bookstore, greeting staff and signing copies of her book in stock. She gave a very entertaining speech that evening and settled in to sign books. There was a long line and, because she is so very prolific, lots of books to sign. As the line wound down, our author started to falter. She was so tired, she didn't think she could continue. Intensely aware of the last few people in line who had patiently waited for so long, I coaxed, cajoled and encouraged her to hang on just a little longer. Eventually everyone got his books signed, and I got her back to her hotel so she could collapse in peace.

Now it's possible our girl was just a wilting flower by nature and would have run out of steam at that point no matter what she had been doing that day. But it certainly set my teeth on edge to think that she had made the trip on the library's dime and then found herself too tired to meet her obligations due to her extracurricular activities. Nor was I thrilled that the bookstores, moneymaking enterprises all, got this bonus without contributing one whit to bringing the author out. Now, doing drive-bys is a common way to fill an author's time during a book tour paid for by the publisher, but a paid appearance is a different matter. I didn't think it was appropriate then, I don't think so now.

I was aggravated enough that I complained to her agent, explaining that I thought it only fair that as we had paid for her client to come she should do for us and nobody else. The agent's response was somewhere between steely and hostile. She thought we were darned lucky to get her at all and, by the way; her price was going up next month. Sheesh.

After that experience, I made sure that we had an exclusivity clause in any contract we made with an author.

Contracts and Agreements

If money changes hands, you need a paper record. If you're working with an agent, they'll send you a contract. It'll look something like this:

Ace Author Agency

CONTRACT #: WKL091406

SPONSOR: King County Library System

SPEAKER: Emily Bronte

DATE OF APPEARANCE: Thursday, January 26, 2006

TIME: 7:30 P.M.

PROGRAM: Emily Bronte will give a 60-minute reading, followed by 20–30 minutes of audience questions. A book signing will follow.

PLACE: Meydenbauer Center (800 seats)

OTHER: All other activities must be cleared through our office before being scheduled.

No lecture or program or any part thereof is to be reproduced, including but not limited to the reproduction by broadcasting, video-taping or tape-recording, without the written permission of the Agency or Speaker.

Sponsor agrees to pay Agency as consideration for the Speakers' services the amount set forth under TERMS below. Payment shall be made 5 DAYS BEFORE THE DATE OF APPEARANCE BY the Speaker and mailed to: ACE AUTHOR AGENCY, 123 Literary Lane, Lilliwaup, WA 98999. The tax ID number for Ace Author Agency is 12345678. Check should be made payable to Ace Author Agency.

TERMS: A fee of $6,000, inclusive of travel and accommodations. Sponsor will also provide all necessary ground transportation.

It is understood that this Contract is binding on both parties; it cannot be cancelled except as follows: The Agency and Sponsor mutually agree that either party may cancel this contract and all parties shall be

---

released from any liability or damages hereunder. If the Speaker or Sponsor is unable to fulfill the terms of this contract due to an act of God or any legitimate conditions beyond the control of the Speaker or Sponsor. However, it is agreed by both parties that best efforts will be made by both parties to so adapt that the lecture be presented as scheduled.

CONTACT(S): Chapple Langemack
Senior Managing Librarian
Bellevue Regional Library
1111 110th Avenue NE
Bellevue, WA 98104
Tel: 425.450.1765

The representative of the Sponsor, in signing this Contract, warrants that (s)he signs as a duly authorized representative of the Sponsor and does not assume personal liability. The Agency has expressed authority to sign on behalf of the Speaker.

Your signed copy of the Contract is acknowledgement that Speaker has accepted this engagement and has agreed to appear at the time and place specified above. The ACE AUTHOR AGENCY reserves the right to withdraw this offer should this contract not be mailed within thirty (30) days of the date "entered into."

This Contract is governed by the laws of the State of Washington and cannot be changed except in writing and signed by both parties.

BY:_____   BY:_____
       (Sponsor)   (Ace Author Agency)

Please sign all four copies of this Contract, retain one copy and return the other three copies to the ACE AUTHOR AGENCY, 123 Literary Lane, Lilliwaup, WA 98999.

Sponsor should consider this contract the invoice for fees due.

If you are working directly with the author, you still need some record. You need to report those earnings to the IRS for one thing, so you'll need the author's social security number. It need not be terribly complicated, however. Here's a sample:

April 5, 2006
Joshua Ortega
1111 11th Ave NE #101
Seattle, WA 98115

Dear Josh,

I am delighted you will be able to do the following programs for the King County Library System:

- January 10 at Federal Way Regional at 2 P.M.

- January 24 at Vashon Library at 2 P.M.

- January 31 at Burien Library at 2 P.M.

As we agreed, King County Library System will pay $XXX.XX for your travel and time. Enclosed is the invoice we will need from you to be able to process your check. Please return it to us at your convenience. An envelope is enclosed.

Cordially,

Chapple Langemack
Reader's Services Coordinator
King County Library System

December 18, 2006

Invoice

King County Library System

Author Appearance

Please make check payable to: Joshua Ortega

Social Security/Tax ID Number: _____

Send to the following address:
1111 11th Ave NE #101
Seattle WA 98115

Total fees to be paid by the King County Library System: $XXX.XX

Signature _____ Date _____

Printed Name_____

More often than not when you're working with a publisher, it'll be a book tour and you won't need to deal with the money aspect. If it turns out you are offering an honorarium, then you need to develop an agreement similar to the one above.

My Friends of the Library have a very streamlined form that they use when money changes hands, which you'll find on the following page. It's basically a tool for the treasurer to know what's going on but all the key ingredients are included.

So the basic techniques here are similar:

To clarify your expectations, put it in writing. If money changes hands, put it in writing. It's always the best practice and will serve you well in the long run.

Bellevue Friends of the Library

Bellevue Regional Library   1111 110th Avenue N.E.   Bellevue, WA 98004

CLAIM FOR REIMBURSEMENT

Speaker's Invoice

Program title _____

Date(s) of program _____

Fee due _____

Check to be made out to: _____

Speaker's name (please print)

Social Security Number/Tax ID #

Address: _____

_____

Date: _____

Submit check to: _____

Date Paid

7

Planning the Event

Author events are all about planning. The more you plan, the more can you anticipate bumps and alternatives, the more likely it is your event will go smoothly. There are so many things to think about and keep track of when you're doing an author event that it's really helpful to have a checklist. On the following page is a checklist we developed over time for single events in a branch library. Take a look and see if you can adapt it to your needs. Then we'll delve into some of the items on the checklist in more detail.

Author Event Checklist

Up to Six Months before the Event

- ☐ Book author
- ☐ Book room to be used
- ☐ Send invoice/letter of confirmation
- ☐ Request press kit
- ☐ Arrange for book sales
- ☐ Negotiate publicity deadlines with Community Relations Department
- ☐ Vet mailing list to determine numbers
- ☐ Determine what phone number to use "for more information"
- ☐ Reserve display cabinet and order books to use in library display, if appropriate
- ☐ Let selection librarian(s) know that the author is coming

Two Months before the Event

- ☐ Reconfirm with author or publisher
- ☐ Write and submit copy for publicity
- ☐ Prepare for mailing flyers, sending e-mails for publicity
- ☐ Double-check on room availability
- ☐ Reconfirm with bookseller

Two to Four Weeks before the Event

- ☐ Reconfirm with author or publisher, add final schedule, directions and contact information. Check for special needs.
- ☐ If payment is involved, submit check request
- ☐ Reconfirm with bookseller
- ☐ Determine room configuration and staffing for event
- ☐ Create displays in the library for the event
- ☐ Purchase—or gather—Post-Its, pens, water
- ☐ Create or revise evaluation form

Day of the Event

- ☐ Set up room: chairs; table for bookseller; podium, microphone and water for speaker; signing table with pens and Post-Its
- ☐ Reserve parking place for author
- ☐ Prepare introduction

After the Event

- ☐ Thank you to author
- ☐ Follow-up to publisher
- ☐ Thank you to venue, if other than library
- ☐ Review evaluations

Venue

You decided before you made your pitch to an author or publisher where you were going to have the event. The checklist told you to book the room in a timely manner. However, you'll also want to give some thought to how this place is going to work for you. If the room you plan to use is in your building, even if it's the room you always use for programs, go in and take a look with a fresh eye. If the venue is somewhere else, make arrangements to go there spend some time taking a really good look and asking questions.

Capacity

What's the capacity of the room? If it's a theatre, with fixed seating, that's pretty easy to determine. If it's an empty room, how many chairs will it hold? How many chairs are available to you? If there aren't as many chairs as you need, how will you get the extras? Who will be setting up the chairs, you or someone at the hosting venue? How many people does the fire department say should be in there? What will you do with an overflow crowd? If you expect multitudes, is it possible to set up monitors in the lobby for additional viewing?

Judi in Florida has the happy problem of almost always having an overflow crowd for "Bookmania!" She now sets up tents and a plasma screen in the library's courtyard so that folks who couldn't get a seat, or who are taking a break from the proceedings, can sit and have a bite to eat and still keep track of what's going on. She hopes eventually to do another simulcast in the County Administration Building next door.

Sightlines

What are the sightlines like? In a theatre the audience seating is often raked, sloping up so that all audience members can see over the person in front of them. If you're dealing with a flat floor, how will people see the speaker? Is there a dais or raised platform you can use? Will your presenter be standing at a podium, or are you having a panel discussion with several authors seated at a table? Remember that it's much harder to see a seated speaker from a flat auditorium floor. If your speaker and the audience are all on the same level, make a note to set up the rows slightly off kilter to one another. You want the person behind looking between heads, not directly at someone else's neck.

Acoustics

How about sound? What are the acoustics of the room like? Is there amplification available? If so, is it a wireless microphone or a stationary stand-up mike? Test it out if you can. It may be a system that hasn't been used in years and really doesn't function well anymore. I think it's always a good idea to have a microphone. You never know if your speaker is a boomer or a whisperer. And given the fact that the population is aging and young people are steadily losing their hearing due to prolonged exposure to loud music, it's just a good idea. (By the way, if I can hear the spill from your headphones, you are not only annoying me, you are damaging your hearing. Just thought you'd like to know.) If a mike setup is not available at the venue, find a system you can borrow or rent. If you're having several speakers in a panel discussion format, remember that you'll need a system that can accommodate several microphones. Check out anything that's likely to give you ambient noise. I can't tell you how many library meeting rooms there are that have perfect acoustics when it comes to the toilets flushing and the hand dryers blowing in the restrooms next door. There's not much you can do about that, but you can warn the speaker—and make arrangement for amplification … of the speaker, not the toilets. Bear in mind that sound in an empty room is much different from sound in a room full of hot bodies. You'll get a lot of echoes and sound bounce in an empty room. Bodies absorb sound, so you'll get much less of that.

Ventilation

Speaking of bodies and their effect on a room, what's the ventilation like? Do you have any control, or is it all automatic? Three hundred bodies produce a lot of heat, 3,000 bodies produce even more. If your program is going to be on a hot day in July, is there air-conditioning? How noisy is it? This will impact your speaker's ability to be heard. If the HVAC system coming to life sounds like a 747 coming in for a landing, you're in trouble.

I have almost fond memories of working in a community theatre housed in an old fruit warehouse. An old, un-air-conditioned fruit warehouse. There were two sure things about summer in this place. One was that temperatures would often reach 100 degrees and more. Two was that the community theatre would produce a summer musical like "Fiddler on the Roof" or "1776" that requires volumnious, preferably woolen, costumes. Ventilation consisted of a couple of swamp coolers perched high in the back of the auditorium. Swamp coolers basically push air through water for a cooling effect. I'm sure the march of progress has improved swamp cooler technology these days, but back then, when you turned on the air, you pretty much came to the conclusion the roof of the building was going to come off. Pity the poor actor trying to make himself heard over that. Needless to say, ventilation was only available before curtain and at intermission. But I digress. Whatever the state of your venue's cooling or heating system, it's a good idea to check it out beforehand so that you know what you're dealing with.

Lighting

Find out what lighting is available to you and where the switchplate or the control panel is. If you're operating in a basic meeting room, you may not have many options. In a theatre, you'll probably have the option of bringing the house lights down or darkening the audience seating during a presentation. This makes for a very dramatic atmosphere and gives the audience members a visual cue to quiet down and pay attention. It also makes it very difficult for the speaker to see the audience, especially if he is lit by bright theatrical lighting. This may or may not be an issue for your speaker; it's best to check beforehand and see if he has any preferences. If a speaker is accustomed to reading the faces of her audience as she goes along, then she'll want at least some light on the audience. If she is content with auditory cues—laughs, sighs, snores or whatever—then a darkened house should be fine.

Setup

When you're getting the venue ready for your program, the most important thing is to give yourself enough time and enough help. It really doesn't signal a warm welcome to your author if he walks in and discovers you hurriedly putting out chairs. Once an author is on your premises you want to give her your attention and meet any needs she may have. Most authors I've hosted are pretty easy, but I have had to scramble a time or two getting coffee or a soft drink.

I'll never forget walking into a library to give a program myself and finding the meeting room locked and dark. None of the staff knew I was coming or was even aware of the program. Not only did it make me feel distinctly unwelcome, it gave me a very good clue as to how much effort had been put into publicity for the event. If the staff didn't even know about it, how did the public stand a chance?

If you've done a thorough investigation of your venue prior to the event, then setup shouldn't hold too many surprises. You've got a few basic things to think about when you're setting up a room for a program. Here's what you need:

- A place for the author. I generally use a podium. If I have a panel, then I set up a table and chairs. Although that the last authors' panel we took a different tack and set up four big upholstered chairs with end tables between each pair. Then we added water and a thermos of coffee on each end table. The authors loved it. I got many comments about what a comfortable atmosphere it created. Make sure there's a banner with your library's logo on the podium or behind the table—especially if BookTV is coming! If I need to improve sightlines, I use a dais. I request this early from the building maintenance guys.

- Water for the author at the podium. And while you're at it, you might as well have an extra bottle or two for you and the bookseller.

- A place for the audience. Set up just enough chairs and leave a stack in the back of the room in case you need them. A smaller crowd seems more palatable if the speaker doesn't have to look out at a sea of empty chairs. Recognize that most people won't sit in the front three rows unless compelled. Not having rows and rows of empty seats in the back compels them. Remember to leave an aisle down the middle—or a couple of aisles if you're dealing with a big group.

- A place for the bookseller. The bookseller will likely need a couple of tables. She'll have a big stack of books to display plus all the ac-coutrements of retail—cash register, credit card machine, sacks. There's a great possibility she'll need power, so place her near an outlet or have an extension cord or power strip on hand. Some book-sellers have banners identifying their store that need to be hung off the table or the wall behind them.

- A place for book signing. Where you'll put the author for book sign-ing after he speaks bears consideration. Under normal circum-stances, I set up a table next to the bookseller, and the author goes there after his remarks to sign, but I have also done it a number of other ways. One way is to put a table at the front of the room next to the podium. When the author is done, he simply moves to the table (where there are pens and more water) and sits to sign. This is an es-pecially effective technique for popular authors. The bookseller is set up at the other end of the room so you have room for the line (more about crowd control in Chapter 10). Another time I set up the signing table next to the bookseller in the hallway because I thought

I'd need every speck of space in the meeting room for chairs and people. I was right about space, but it became difficult to escort the popular author through the room out to the book signing table. People came up to her en route to chat or have their books signed and I had to run a lot of interference.

- When the event is in a theatre, I set up the bookseller and the signing table in the lobby. This works particularly well in the theatre that we use because there's a back passageway from the stage to the lobby and I can escort the author out without running a gauntlet of fans. The lobby allows plenty of room for a queue.

- A place for refreshments. To my mind, refreshments are purely optional for author events. Christina, a Swedish friend of mine, always says, "Oh, you Americans. You have to eat at every occasion." It depends on the feeling you want, the time of day and the size of crowd you expect. Judy from Utah likes to set a table with coffee, cookies and fresh flowers. She thinks it gives the event a special occasion feel. Plus, one of the goals of Judy's programs is that members of the community gather and chat with one another. Refreshments help that to happen. We often do a table with coffee and treats for a cozy feeling, but it was absolutely mandatory when we did an event for Bharti Kirchner's book *Pastries*.

- Also take some time prior to the event and fill a box or basket with things that you'll need during the program. Tuck in pens and Post-Its for the signing, a couple of bottles of water, your evaluation forms, your introduction, the book that you have set aside to get signed and a camera. Then you'll be all ready to go and won't have to think very hard if things get frantic.

Those are the basics of planning the logistics for your author event. You may want to put a flyer advertising your next event on every seat or have a stack of program calendars at the door. You can add as many extras as you want. It's also nice if you can have a poster on an easel outside the front door to identify the location (and maybe snag some extra bodies in the audience). But basically, as long as you've got a spot for the author, audience and bookseller, you're in good shape.

8

Promoting Your Event

Ah, promotion. If ever there was a bugaboo in author events, this is it. My heart sinks when a patron comes into the library and exclaims, "You had Phillipa Gregory here last Thursday! If only I had known I would surely have come." We all have busy lives, and that affects not only the time we have to come to programs such as author events but also the way we get—and retain—information about such things. I don't know about you, but I can walk by a poster and get all hyped up about attending an event and then forget all about it by the time I reach my destination. So I think the key to publicity is repetition and the use of as many avenues as possible. Here's a case study:

Getting the Word Out

I have a library card for the small town where I live, but I don't often visit the library. Let's face it, I work in a library all day long, I pretty much have all the library access I need on the job. Also, like many people, I have a fair commute. Once I get home and out of my work duds, I am disinclined to go out again.

My home library system sponsors county-wide author events. Often, these events take place in my town. These events are cosponsored by the county's independent bookstores and the daily newspaper. Now even though I rarely darken the door of my hometown library, I know about and often attend these events. How can this be?

When I stroll around town to shop and run errands, I see posters advertising the event in nearly every store window. The graphic on the poster remains the same throughout the series, so I recognize it instantly as an author event. When I go to the bookstore to buy gifts for my nieces (ah, the curse of having a librarian for an aunt!), there is a big display featuring the author that is coming to town, even though the event is not happening in the bookstore. The grocery store promotes the event on its readerboard, and I see that as I walk by or drive through town. I'm a ferry commuter, so I notice each day on my way to work that there is an advertisement for the event posted on the bulletin board in the ferry terminal and on the boat itself. Surfing through channels on television in the evening I see a video "bulletin board" notice for the event on the local access cable channel. There is also a broadcast of previous author events in the series. Our local weekly newspaper has a big article about the author a week or two before the event. The regional daily newspaper, one of the sponsors, has several articles on the author and the program. As I scan through the metropolitan weekly newspaper looking for restaurant and theatre reviews, I notice that the author event is listed in the calendar section under "Readings and Literary Events." I get an e-mail from a friend who tells me about the event. She's very excited because the author is one of her favorites and happens to be very attractive. (Words have that effect on some of us.) She contemplates the best way to get his attention—should she bring heavenly food to the event? Dress provocatively? (Oh, woe those extra pounds.) Or perhaps just throw her house key up to the podium? By now, I am not only aware of the event, I can remember the date and time. It's planned for Sunday afternoon at the school auditorium not far from my house. Sunday afternoon is a most civilized time in my opinion. At our library, it's the busiest day of the week. If I'm not working, I've worn out my weekend ambitions by then and am ready to relax and be engaged. As it happens, my mother-in-law is visiting that weekend, so we all go to hear the author and have a fine time. As did about 300 other people.

My home library did everything right in publicizing this event and reaped the reward in attendance. The event was part of an ongoing series and had a consistent and readily recognizable graphic. I knew the instant I saw the photo of the wicker rocker on the porch that an author was coming to town. They used every avenue of publicity open to them, from posters in shop windows to the grocery store readerboard to the standard media. Beyond publicity, they got the basics right. They chose an author of interest to their community and a time and day that was convenient for their commuter population.

The key things to remember about publicity are timing, repetition and range of media. Remember that if your author is coming on a book tour, his publicist is making arrangements for publicity. If it's up to you, then do your homework and figure out how many publicity avenues are available to you. Be imaginative when you're thinking about publicity venues. Fern Reiss gives good advice to authors in her book *The Publishing Game: Bestseller in 30 Days*. If your author has written a book about fishing, don't limit yourself to bookstores, go where the fishermen are—bait shops, sporting good stores, boat shops. The same applies to your author event. Think who you audience is and go after them where they might be.

Once you've identified the avenues of publicity you want to pursue, find out who the contacts are and when you need to get information to them to meet their deadline. Maybe it's Larry at the grocery store who decides what messages go up on the readerboard. Find out what kind of event Larry gives priority to, how far in advance he wants to know about your shindig and how he wants to receive the information.

Sit down and do a calendar that includes each medium you'll be using for publicity. Work backward from the date of the event and set a deadline for each medium. If the posters need to be up in store windows three weeks before the event, when does the copy for the posters need to be in to the printer? If you want to make sure the Audubon Society has the information about David Sibley's visit to promote *The Sibley Guide to Birds,* then find out the deadline for their newsletter. How far in advance does the newspaper need items for the events calendar? You get the idea.

Working with the Media

If you are in charge of getting the word out about your author events, you'll need to build and nurture your relationships with the media. Jan Thenell, retired director of public relations for Multnomah County Library in Portland, Oregon, advises librarians looking to get the word out to pay attention to the media around them. "Read, listen to, watch, and log on to local, regional and national media," says Jan, "and read your local daily newspaper religiously; it often sets the agenda for the other media in your community." Watch for reporter bylines, editorials and op-ed pieces so you begin to learn the players in the news world.

Let's look at some of the specific media individually.

Newspaper

How much luck you have getting a mention in the newspaper might have a lot to do with how big your community is and how big your library is. My experiences with small-town newspapers have been quite wonderful. In a small community, it's pretty darn easy to wander across the street and make the acquaintance of the editor and the reporters. My favorite small weekly newspaper was the *Huckleberry Herald.* There was an editor (who was also the photographer), a part-time reporter and an office manager. It wasn't too hard to know who had the library beat. I made it a practice to stop in and chat briefly from time to time even when I didn't have a story. When I did have a story or a photo opportunity, it was easy to let them know. The other great thing was that everybody in town read *The Huckleberry* so you were sure of getting the word out. It was great fun.

Now I work in a big library in a big library system, and we tend to overwhelm the daily metropolitan papers with everything we have going on. The listing for storytimes alone in forty-three libraries is enormous. Our Community Relations Department does what it can to find clever approaches to promote our programs but often "library" doesn't seem to engender much enthusiasm in the big-city press. We get a lot of coverage for a computer hacker or a censorship flap, but other than that we really have to work at it. I can still wander across the street to the branch office of the big daily and chat with a columnist about library doings. Or I can e-mail a note to a reporter that I know is interested in library affairs. The personal touch is still an effective one.

A good rule to bear in mind when you're dealing with newspapers is to make it as easy as you can for them. Reporters are busy folk; they're under deadline, and they may not have time to come up to speed with the background knowledge needed for a story. If you can do it for them, you're ahead of the game. Think of an interesting approach to your event. Write a snappy, professional press release. Have digital photos available. Back in the old days, when I was dealing with a small-city daily newspaper, I was told by one editor (with a certain amount of 'tude, I might add) that I could submit a press release about a library program but that staff rewrote everything. Hmmm. I submitted a press release, and it ran untouched, word for word, just as I had written it.

My Friends of the Library gnash their teeth when one of their events doesn't make it into the paper, and they desperately want to march over to the newspaper office and demand an explanation. It's hard to accept the fact that the newspaper may not have the time, space or interest to run your story, but you must. Do your best, stay positive, keep lines of communication open and make as many personal contacts as you can, but don't expect publicity miracles from the newspaper. The rule is: if you absolutely, positively must have your message in the newspaper, buy advertising.

Here's a bare bones but effective press release I received by e-mail:

October 25, 2005

FOR IMMEDIATE RELEASE

SEATTLE PUBLIC LIBRARY & UNIVERSITY BOOK STORE
PRESENT

E. L. DOCTOROW

PLEASE NOTE: Due to his National Book Award nomination, E. L. Doctorow has had to reschedule his appearance from November 18 to December 13. We congratulate Mr. Doctorow on the nomination.

EVENT: E. L. Doctorow reads from and signs *The March* (Random House)

DATE/TIME: Tuesday, December 13, 2005, 7 P.M.

LOCATION: Seattle Public Library, Central Branch, 1000 Fourth Ave., Seattle

PHONE FOR PUBLIC: 206-634-3400

CONTACT: Stesha Brandon or Jim Brimble, 206-634-3400

DETAILS: *The March* follows William Tecumseh Sherman's bloody advance through Georgia to the sea, retold with the power and style of one of America's great novelists. To paraphrase reviewer Walter Kirn, when you already know how a story ends, the middle better be good. And trust E. L. Doctorow to deliver the goods with this powerful, sweeping and compassionate historical novel.

Sponsored by University Book Store and Seattle Public Library.

SPONSORS: Seattle Public Library and University Book Store

ADMISSION: Free

(The ### is press release code for "this is the end.")

If you want to go beyond bare-bones facts, or maybe embroider your facts a little, there are tons of good books on publicity out there that will tell you in depth how to write a press release. I was particularly impressed by this excerpt from "Publicty 101" by Claudia O'Keefe that originally appeared in the June/July 2005 issue of *American Libraries*:

Anatomy of a Compelling Press Release

Want to know how to write a compelling event-oriented press release? Simple—read the arts section of any newspaper until you find an article that has you hauling out your day planner and penciling in the event described. Although a press release is technically a different animal than a news story, both follow the same format and conventions.

Just as a reporter searches for a dynamic opening line to hook a reader into reading his or her story, you too should look for an enticing first sentence or paragraph. Sure, you can always start your press release with a dull recitation of facts, the what-where-when of the thing. It's not only possible, but probable that many small-town newspapers will still print your news even if you start your release with something like this:

"On February 18 at 7:30 P.M., the Zucchini County Public Library welcomes noted throat specialist Dr. David Dudenhoffer, who will discuss the many causes of excess phlegm."

Even if a paper were to print this release word for word, how many ordinary librarygoers do you suppose will be lining up to hear Dudenhoffer speak when the event sounds like a medical symposium?

Granted, there aren't many ways to make phlegm sound enticing. Yet even with a subject as difficult as this to promote, it's possible to humanize it, to make it more immediate and intriguing. Try this:

"Ever had a frog in your throat and wondered how it got there? Noted specialist Dr. David Dudenhoffer will be happy to answer this and any other ticklish questions you might have about throats when he speaks on the subject at the Zucchini County Public Library, February 18 at 7:30 P.M."

Notice that I don't include the word phlegm anywhere in my opening paragraph? It wasn't necessary because the second paragraph is where I really dive into the specifics of the upcoming presentation. Here's where I make my case for the event, why it will be of special interest and use to you—the person reading my press release—to get in your car and drive to the library to look at slides of diseased throats.

By paragraph three I'm launching into a brief bio on the good doctor, about the book he's written on his favorite topic, phlegm, and what motivated him to publish it. By paragraph four or five, I've finished with the doctor and am moving into the nitty-gritty of the event, any miscellaneous but still important facts I wasn't able to fit into my opening paragraphs (i.e., how long the talk will last, whether it's free to the public, or if refreshments will be served).

Hopefully you're observing a pattern here in how I've structured my release. It's known as the upside-down pyramid method: I put the most important facts at the top of the release and gradually work my way down through the information, inserting it in order of importance until I reach my final paragraph—the one with all the leftovers only the most dedicated reader will want to know.

This is where you mention your sponsors as a way to thank them for their financial assistance, as well as any state or federal agencies that also provided support. Your last paragraph is where you will see one of the most obvious differences between a real news story and a press release. A news story is news, pure news. A press release is a news story with an agenda.

What's the very last line of an event-driven press release? "For more information about this or any other library event, contact the Zucchini County Public Library at 304-555-ZUKE, or visit us on the web at www.zucchinilibrary.org." Naturally, you'll want to change this to your own library's phone number and web address, and perhaps add the name of a contact person.

Note: Reprinted with permission of *American Libraries.*

I've also included some useful sources for writing press releases and dealing with the media in general in the Additional Resources section in the back of this book.

Radio

The great thing about radio is its immediacy. I have had patrons show up to an event because they happened to hear the author being interviewed while they were in their car.

Public Service Announcements (or PSAs) used to be the bread and butter of the nonprofit world. You had some hope that your fifteen- or thirty-second spot would be read in the spirit of service to the community. Market pressures seem to have driven out most of that particular custom, even in the 2 A.M. time slot. There is still some mention of community calendar events on some stations. Again, do your research to find out how the station prefers to get that information.

And then there's talk radio. If your author is well known or has an interesting topic, it may be possible to have her interviewed on your local "all news" or "all talk" station. For this you'll need good timing and the cooperation of the author. An interview that airs after your event doesn't do you much good. An author may be able and willing to do a phone interview the day before from wherever he might happen to be.

Many libraries report happy partnerships with their local public radio station. (Maybe it's that whole nonprofit bonding thing.) So that's another channel you should investigate. One event planner says that she buys 100 PSAs on her local public radio station as her sole paid advertising because that's the best match for her audience.

Television

Like radio, television is a tough nut to crack anymore. Your best bet is locally produced news and lifestyle shows. Local access cable may also be an option. Like I mentioned earlier, my hometown local access cable channel broadcasts author events live and repeats them at regular intervals. The tapes of these events are also available to check out from the library.

Don't think that the news media is your only ticket to getting your message out. Publishing your own newsletters, brochures and Web site allows you to control both the message and manner of presentation.

BookTV and Me

Judi from Florida had a terrific experience with CSpan's BookTV. In preparing for her "Bookmania!" program, she noticed that BookTV now has a bus that travels the country to book fairs and festivals, bookstores and libraries. They were slated to be in her area at the right time, so she contacted them and sent off the slate of nonfiction authors that would be attending her event. They not only came, they stayed for the whole event and ended up putting three segments on nationally.

Internet

I think it's almost a given that every agency has its own Web page these days. Our library's Web site is a great one and is heavily accessed by our users. As a matter of fact, when we tell an author's publicist that we get 9 million hits a month on our Web page, we can practically hear her jaw drop. That's a lot of exposure, and it gets people's attention. Authors have also been swayed into visiting us by the popularity of our Web site.

Ready, Set, Web!

Get with your webmaster and plan your course of action for an author event. First of all come up with a URL—like www.kcls.org/authors—that is easy for patrons, staff and authors to remember. If they can remember it, they may remember to check in on it from time to time. Now it's time for logistics. Consider the following:

Timing and Geography

When do you want a notice to appear on the site, and where will it be? How many clicks will it take to get there? Will the notice move to the front page? If so, when?

Copy and Graphics

Who will write the copy? Be sure that it's written in the format that your webmaster needs. Ideally, the same copy will appear on your print materials as well. Prepare an abbreviated version, if necessary, for the front page. What will you use for a graphic? Generally the publisher will provide a graphic of the book jacket and a photo of the author in electronic format. Check to make sure it's the right format for your Web site. Your best bet is to use what the publisher provides. Some authors are very particular about what photos are used. Also, Lisa, our webmaster, wants you to know that if you pull any old graphic off the Web, you could get into some serious trouble. Again, use the same graphic on the Web that you use for your print pieces.

Linking

Decide if there will there be links to any other Web sites in conjunction with this event. You'll likely want to link to the authors books in your catalog so that your patrons can request his books easily. You may wish to link to the author's own Web page or the Web site of the publisher. If you are cosponsoring this event with another agency, you may wish to provide a link to its Web site as well. Consider if you want to give viewers the option of linking to other author events you have planned for the future—or at other libraries in your system.

The main thing is to figure it all out so your webmaster has adequate advance notice. Do what's necessary to make it smooth and easy for her. If it's easy, it's more likely to happen. And don't forget to thank her for her help!

Electronic Reminders

The other great use of the Internet is to remind people via e-mail that the event is coming up. That's a great technique, especially to reach busy folk who are tied to their computers. At each author event, we provide cards so that people who wish to be notified of upcoming author events can give us their e-mail address.

It's a good idea to ask your patrons to add your webmaster to their "allowed" list. Internet service providers like AOL and Earthlink give their members the option of receiving e-mail only from specified addresses. If you are not on the list, your message will end up in the junk mail pile with all the offers of Viagra and Rolex watches. This is also an issue if your library sends overdues or hold notices via e-mail. Make sure you use a recognizable address, for instance, King County Library System Webmaster, rather than KCLS Webmaster. Also make sure that the names of the library and the author appear in the subject line.

Never send an e-mail to a patron without his or her permission. It's a breach of privacy and just plain bad policy. If you are sending folks unsolicited e-mails, how do they know what else you're doing with their e-mail address? In the same vein, if you are using Microsoft Outlook, make sure you put everyone in the bcc, blind carbon copy, field. Just because your patrons have asked to hear about author events doesn't necessarily mean they want the world to know that or have access to their e-mail address.

Webmaster Lisa suggests using a third-party mailing system. Topica, for example, makes it easy to design a nice-looking newsletter. It also offers seamless online sign-ups.

From time to time we would get a phone call from a very irritated patron complaining that he had received an unsolicited e-mail (or postcard) from us promoting an author event. Almost always, when we led him through the process that we used to gain addresses for reminders, he would remember that he had indeed been to an author event previously and had filled out the form. It's a good idea, however, to provide an easy "unsubscribe" feature so that a patron can easily take himself off the list.

We send out a message a couple of weeks before the event and again a couple of days before the author program. If you set up a VCS file, folks can easily add it to their Outlook calendar. We don't require registration or tickets for our programs, but if you do, it would be nice to offer that ability online as well.

I see that some libraries are taking this one step further and offering patrons RSS feeds so that they can be immediately notified of author events and other library doings.

The Unpromotion of an Event

One Friday night before her Saturday Bookmania! event, Judi thought she would check her voicemail at work one more time. What she heard was a frantic message from the publicist for her main speaker the following night. Olivia Goldsmith, author of *The First Wives Club*, had been injured in a fall and would not be able to appear. Now it was Judi's turn to be frantic. She spent the night and most of the next day making phone calls to the press and everyone else she could think of to whom she could spread the word about the program's cancellation.

Saturday night at the appointed time, Judi trudged to the venue, apology speech in hand. There was no one there. Absolutely no one. Judi wonders to this day if no one really wanted to hear Olivia Goldsmith or if she was just a smashingly successful unpublicist.

Print Pieces

At our last author event, a good two-thirds of the audience came clutching the flyer we had put out in the library. Give some thought to the kind and number of print pieces you produce. Consider where you will put them. How much room do you have? Will they lie on a counter, or will they need to fit into some kind of holder? A straight 8½ x 11-inch sheet may work just fine for you. This format can also be easily enlarged to 11 x 17-inch for a poster. Maybe you'd like to do a bookmark that staff can put in books as they check people out and that are small enough to stash by the self-checkout stations. Don't forget you can put them in the author's books on the shelf as well. Think of how a piece can serve more than one purpose. If you produce 4 x 6-inch postcard-size pieces, you can use them as flyers in the library and mail them out to your potential audience. An 8½ x 11-inch piece can be folded over or be trifolded and be mailed out as well, but it's sometimes harder to get enough attention-grabbing copy on the outside of the piece.

Here's a sample timeline for a print piece used by Jane Graham George at Dakota County Library in Minnesota:

Timeline for Brochure Completion

Description	Deadline Date
Authors contacted and booked (i.e., mail contracts)	5/17
Request color scheme samples from printer	5/24
Verify that all information from signed contract is the same as that on the brochure	5/24
Draft brochure (proofread twice)	5/28
Draft poster (proofread twice)	5/28
Brochure draft to printer	6/09
Brochure approval to printer (FINAL)	6/30
Brochures in hand to distribute to public	7/28
Posters in hand to distribute to branches for display	7/28

You may wish to add in deadlines for having the copy written and the design and artwork for your brochure completed and approved if that's how it works in your organization.

Direct Mail

I love it when I can do direct mail for an event. Sending a postcard about an event to an entire zip code is work and has a certain cost, but it can attract people who didn't even know there was a library in town.

Here's a sample of copy you can use for a postcard:

Meet the Author!

Claire Krulikowski, author of *Moonlight on the Ganga*

Visiting India to explore the marvels of the Ganga River, Claire Krulikowski finds herself face to face with a leper, an ill stalker, an electrocuted wild monkey and poverty beyond American comprehension. These experiences contribute to the most powerful spiritual awakening of her life. Join Claire Krulikowski as she discusses India's spiritual impact and shares her experiences embracing a foreign culture and renewed spirit.

Kirkland Library on Wednesday, July 18 at 7:30 P.M.
    308 Kirkland Avenue; Kirkland, WA

Fairwood Library on Thursday, June 28 at 7 P.M.
    17009 140th Avenue SE; Renton, WA

Covington Library on Tuesday, July 24 at 7 P.M.
    27100 –164th Avenue SE; Covington, WA

For more information call 425.369.3318 or check kcls.org

As I mentioned previously, we always collect e-mail or street addresses from audience members who want to be notified of upcoming author events. I think this works particularly well to help build an audience in a series. We started one interview series with well-known authors to draw a crowd and dutifully collected address information. The next year we included some authors who were not so well known but still interesting speakers. I wanted the audience to come along with me, to invest the time in these authors they'd never heard of, so I sent out a letter via e-mail and U.S. mail to everyone who had expressed interest in being notified of author programs.

---

1 September 2006

Dear Fellow Book Lover,

Enclosed is the line up for this fall's Authors in Conversation series at the Bellevue Regional Library. I'm particularly excited that we have an opportunity to showcase some new voices in fiction.

I was entranced when author Harriet Scott Chessman led me into the world of nineteenth-century Paris and the lives of sisters Mary and Lydia Cassatt in her gem of a novel *Lydia Cassatt Reading the Morning Paper.* I'm so pleased that Harriet will be on hand to talk about life, art and writing on September 30.

Pastries: A Novel of Desserts and Discoveries is author Bharti Kirchner's latest treat. Set in the very recent Seattle past, *Pastries* tells the story of a young woman whose business and love life go awry—and her way back to self and sustenance. It's only right that we round up some tea and pastries to enjoy while we chat with the charming Bharti on October 9.

Seattle in the 1940s was a rip-roaring kind of place according to author Curt Colbert—the perfect place for hard-boiled private detective Jake Rossiter and his able-bodied girl Friday, Miss Jenkins. Colbert's noir mysteries *Rat City* and *Sayonaraville* evoke the golden age of pulp fiction. Curt is a former actor and director who is great fun to talk to. If we can coax him to read aloud, you'll think you've heard tough guy Jake in the flesh. Hear Curt on October 23.

Come and join me at the Bellevue Regional Library for a sneak peak at these talented authors on the rise. You'll be able to say you knew them when. Book sales and signing with follow each event.

Yours in reading,

Chapple Langemack
Readers' Services Coordinator
King County Library System

As I may have mentioned, I live on an island—a pretty easily identified community. To take advantage of that, my hometown library does a quarterly newsletter that is sent to everyone on the island. It has been a very effective publicity piece for them, and it gives me, a resident, a good feeling for what's going on at the library. You don't have to live on an island to take advantage of this concept, however. You can do a broadcast direct mail piece to any zipcode. You can also do multiple zipcodes. You just can't do part of a zipcode.

Display

Don't forget to tout your program in displays throughout the library. Displays can capture attention more readily than a flyer, no matter how artfully produced. Not long ago we were hosting an up-and-coming mystery author at our library. One of our librarians set up a display of her books near the front entrance, heavily salted with flyers promoting the event. Shortly before the event I walked by and noticed two women examining the display with great interest. I stopped to give them encouragement, admiring the display with them. "Isn't it great? She'll be here tonight!" Then I looked up into their faces. It was the author with her escort. Well, it was still great. And the author was quite pleased to be the subject of a display.

We once hosted Melissa Houtte who, with her sister Allison, wrote *Alligators, Old Mink and New Money*, in which vintage clothing plays a starring role. Not only is Melissa bubbly and infectiously charming, she's a woman who knows how to merchandize. She brought bags of clothing to use for her presentation plus a fold-up mannequin that she dressed and posed outside the meeting room. It was great fun, and no one had any doubts as to where the program was.

Community Resources

When you're planning publicity for your event, think about what's available to you outside your library or agency. Maybe it's the readerboard at the grocery store, like in my town. Think about your author and your audience. If I were hosting someone with a particular appeal to women, like Jill Conner Brown, I'd do a booklist of Jill's books plus a few other readalikes with the details of her program on the other side. I'd drop some off at all the places in town that have a large female clientele—hair salons and spas, fabric stores, clothing stores. Anywhere you think there might be Sweet Potato Queen wannabes. The same goes for men, or any particular group for the matter. Think of the natural tie-ins and try some guerilla marketing.

Speaking of groups, make yourself aware of groups and organizations in your community that might have a special interest in your author. I mentioned earlier that the Seattle chapter of the Sons of Ireland were immensely interested in hearing Malachy McCourt and that the garden club likes to cohost writers on gardening. Your local Sherlock Holmes Society might be interested in a mystery author like Laurie King, author of *The Beekeeper's Apprentice* and the rest of the Mary Russell series in which Sherlock Holmes plays a prominent role. When David at Tacoma Public Library hosts a mountain climber who has written about his latest adventure, he makes sure to notify the Mountaineers (a local organization of outdoor enthusiasts), the Sierra Club and any other organization that might be interested. He also makes sure his flyers are at Recreational Equipment (REI) stores and other mountaineering shops. Having a built-in nucleus of folks who are keen on your author or topic is a great way to build an audience.

If you give this some thought and do some research, you may surprise yourself at what you can come up with. Here's a publicity source that surprised me. My library is in a pretty good-sized city, and we have a number of high-rise buildings downtown. Who knew that there was such a thing as a corporate concierge? They serve exactly the same function as a concierge for a hotel with some social director activities thrown in. These are great folk to keep informed of what's going on in your library.

When doing publicity for your program, don't tie yourself to the standard channels. David put it more bluntly: "If you just count on the newspaper, you're dead." One story that deeply impressed me was when a poet told about a visit he made to a small Midwestern town. The town librarian made contact with him and said she was trying to make all the arrangements to have him visit. A year later, she contacted him and said she was still working on it. Two years later, she finally had everything in place. The poet arrived in town for the visit and was dumbstruck to see a poster heralding his visit in every store window in town. When he made his visit to the high school, every student had read his poetry. He spoke at every service club and group in town. Everyone welcomed him. The pièce de résistance? When he pulled into town, there was huge banner across Main Street: "WELCOME NEW YORK CITY POET DAVE JOHNSON!" He was so thrilled he called his mother at 3 A.M. and woke her up to tell her. So think deeply about your community and let your imagination roam and see how you can pinpoint and alert the audience you're looking for.

9

Hosting and Escorting

If you are hosting an author event, then it is incumbent on you to be just that—a gracious host. Do whatever you can to make the author's visit a pleasant one, door to door.

Planes, Trains and Automobiles

Consider how your chosen author is coming to you and how you might make that easier for both of you. If your author is coming by car, send him maps and detailed directions of how to get to your venue at least two weeks in advance. Tell him if there's any funny stuff he needs to know about traffic or construction or other potential obstacles. Reiterate what time you will expect him to appear and who the contact person on site will be if it's not you: "Sue will be there to meet you."

Why do a reminder in two or three weeks as opposed to a week—or two days for that matter? Number one reason is that it's a nice amount of warning time for the author, and he will be able to start thinking about his presentation. Number two reason is that it's a workable amount of time for you should the author have totally forgotten and now be unable to make the gig. Yes, you're shuddering, as well you should. This has happened to me and I can testify that while it's slightly embarrassing to call in another author to pinch hit with two or three weeks notice, it's nowhere near as mortifying as calling two days before the event when neither of you can even pretend the substitute was your first choice. Also consider how long it's going to take you to get the word out about a change of talent or a cancellation. Maybe you'll need more than two or three weeks.

It's also just a good thing to confirm the program. I blush to admit that I discovered the hard way how critical this step is. I booked one noted author months in advance for a series at our library. At that point I figured I knew he was coming and let myself get busy and distracted by other things and didn't follow up as I should have. A week or so before the event, I had an e-mail from one testy author wanting to know if this event was on or not! No matter how much I apologized or worked to soothe the situation, the rocky road was established. It got the point where when I told him I'd put out a pylon to reserve a parking place for him, he retorted that he didn't know what I was talking about. It turns out he was right, a pointy orange thing is a traffic cone, not a pylon, but ay-yi-yi! My carelessness took us to a very bad place.

Roberta Johnson, a librarian and frequent speaker, said the only untoward thing that has happened in her speaking career is when someone discussed the possibility of her doing a program a few months down the road, then never contacted her to confirm or regret the program. "Three days before the discussed date, she called to ask what time I thought I would arrive! I got my act together and did the program, but thought she could have learned a thing or two about follow-up."

A similar thing happened to me last week, only in reverse. The local Kiwanis Club had asked me to come and speak. As the date grew closer, I didn't receive a confirmation or reminder. Finally, on the morning of the meeting, I called the program chair and asked if he still wanted me to come. He dug through his files and reported that I was not on for that date, but for a date in the following month. Now I know that's not the date we had agreed on, but that's a different story. Suffice it to say, follow-up, even several times, is critical.

If your author is coming via plane or train, you can choose to meet her in person or include carfare expenses in her fee. I like to meet my authors at the airport when it's at all possible. I think it gives them a level of comfort and the feeling that they are valued and being taken care of. Plus, it often helps to establish a bond. Remember, this is a stranger in a strange land, and even a grown-up appreciates having a familiar face as a touchstone throughout her visit.

Of course you're no longer able to meet someone at the airport gate, so baggage claim is the most common fallback position. A good trick is to carry a copy of the author's book. That way you don't have to try to identify an author from a publicity photo that may or may not be several years old or describe yourself in minute detail. You can just say, "I'm a tall blonde and I'll have a copy of your book." Believe me, most authors can spot a copy of their book a mile away.

If your author is on book tour, or otherwise visiting under the aegis of a publisher, standard operating procedure is for the publisher to hire a professional media escort. I generally talk with the publicist about transport before plans get set in cement. It's a friendly gesture, and we'll often find that there are times when it's helpful for me to provide transportation and times when it's better to hire an escort. Here's an example: On Monday, a well-known author is coming in to speak at two library systems in two days. She will also be doing some television and radio appearances. The publicist and I agreed that I will pick up the author at the airport, take her to her hotel and then to her first library program, which has some quirky local transportation issues (known as ferries) that I am familiar with. The next day, a professional escort will take her to her media appointments and then deliver her to my library for her appearance. I get the best of both worlds—a chance to chat with the author before our program and release from the hassle of trying to make tight connections with her other commitments.

Anyone responsible for transportation—publicist or author—is glad for any information you can give them beforehand on how long it really takes to get from here to there, especially if there are traffic issues an out-of-towner wouldn't know about.

Also, double-check to see if the author is traveling alone or with a spouse or assistant. I went to the airport to pick up an author one time and found that her assistant was traveling with her. Ooops. We were all good-sized ladies and nobody was traveling light. My two-door coupe was not the ideal transportation. I could have arranged for a different car had I known. Actually, I don't think the publicist knew either because there wasn't an extra room booked at the hotel. Oh, well. The moral to this story is ask, ask and ask again.

Surprise!

Escorting an author is 99.9 percent fun. But there is a reason that professional media escorts say that being unflappable is a key quality for a good escort. One year we hosted Ruby Ann Boxcar just for the fun of it. Ruby Ann is the author of *Ruby Ann's Down Home Trailer Park Cookbook,* among others. To say Ruby Ann is theatrical is an understatement. Ruby Ann is larger than life in every sense of the word. From her rhinestone eyeglasses to her sky-high beehive hairdo, Ruby Ann is an event. Think of Dame Edna and then go south and you've got some idea. (Or you can just go to rubyannboxcar.com and take a gander.)

At any rate, Ruby Ann arrived at the library with a small contingent of boys who were fluffing and patting and fetching (I've got to get me some boys!) and a rather wide-eyed escort. It turns out, no one ever told the escort that Ruby Ann is really a man. Not only that, no one ever told her Ruby Ann's real name. The poor escort presented herself at the hotel and asked for Ruby Ann Boxcar. There wasn't any such person registered there. I would have given anything to see the look on her face when Ruby Ann appeared. It makes me chuckle even now.

Are We There Yet?

If it's up to you to drive your author, whether it's picking him up at the airport or taking him to the performance venue, then remember that you're still a host even while you're a driver. This doesn't mean concentrate on your author to the exclusion of your driving, quite the opposite. Be on your best driving behavior. Do all the good stuff like signaling and driving the speed limit. If you're in a "company" car you'll want to do that anyway.

Also be a good host when it comes to the car environment. Let your guest dictate the temperature—or at least check in with her. I had one speaking engagement in the Midwest in July—a truly daunting experience for a girl accustomed to cool maritime climes. I was all duded up in my presenter clothes when I climbed into my ride's car. My clothes and my spirits both wilted when she breezily announced that she never turned on the air-conditioning. It was a long hot ride, and I arrived to do my big presentation soaked with sweat and effectively de-coiffed by freeway driving with the windows open. Don't do that to your author. On the other hand, I hosted an author one lovely autumn and found that she was a great fan of air-conditioning. By my lights it was quite pleasant, but we had air-conditioning to the point where I'm pretty sure we could have successfully transported frozen food as well (although these days I'm a little more empathetic about that). Remember that great line from the movie *My Favorite Year*? The chauffer driving Peter O'Toole declares, "When I'm driving Mr. Swann, he's chief of the car. And when the chief says he wants to make stops, Alfie Bambacelli makes the stops. And that's what I live by."

Be aware of the noise level as well. It's really not a good time to tune into your favorite radio station, no matter how soothing YOU find it. Your author may want to chat or may just want to rest and gather herself so try to be sensitive to that.

If I'm picking up an author from the airport, I do try to give her an overview of their upcoming program and the library system. It's nice to give her the details about the demographics of the town where the library is and the kind of audience she can expect. You may have gone over this thoroughly with the publicist or agent, but you'd be amazed at how much the author doesn't really know about where she is and why. Also, try to be a little knowledgeable about your area. I never actually thought about how big Lake Washington was until an author asked me. (It's twenty-two miles long, by the way, and encompasses 21,500 acres.)

When planning your itinerary, allow for some wiggle room. You never know if your author will be Johnny-on-the-spot punctual or perpetually tardy, so give yourself and your author a little leeway.

Above all, be professional. Your job is to look after the well-being of your author while getting him where he needs to go. You need to be flexible, personable and sensitive to his needs. You do not need to be his new best friend. Be respectful of his time and personal space. Remember why he is here. Do not ever, ever use this opportunity to quiz a financial author about stocks or an author of best-selling fiction how to get an agent.

Welkommen, Bienvenue, Welcome!

If you've gone to all the trouble of inviting an author and publicizing a program, then for heaven's sake, make sure she feels welcome when she shows up. Here's an example of what a difference a greeting makes:

A Tale of Two Talks

I was invited to speak to the staff of a large insurance company. Diversity training was a big concern for this firm, and they'd asked me to talk about some multicultural titles. The plan was for me to speak at the main office one day and at the branch office the next day. The communications I received from the company's training staff were clear, courteous and concise. I received a confirmation immediately after the date was set, a reminder about two weeks before with a query about my equipment needs, and a friendly, "Looking forward to seeing you tomorrow!" message a day before the event.

I arrived at the main office, was greeted warmly by the receptionist and was sent to park my car in a special guest spot in the garage. I was met and greeted by name by the parking attendant and directed across the sky bridge to meet my escort in the main building. As soon as I entered the building my host greeted me, fixed me up with a nametag and took me to the venue. She made sure the microphone set up was to my liking and offered me any number of beverages, and even lunch. When the presentation was over, she escorted me back to the sky bridge, thanking me profusely. When I arrived in the garage, a new parking attendant, one I'd not seen before, greeted me and asked me what books I'd recommended. Boy was I impressed. I felt like the most important speaker ever.

The next day I looked forward to more superstar treatment at the branch office, which was a sprawling campus on park-like grounds. Checking in at the front desk I was soon given to know that they didn't know who I was, what I was talking about or where I was supposed to speak. Finally I was directed to another part of the campus where I bumped around until I found my room. My host uncoupled himself from a conversation long enough to inform me that he couldn't stay; he had an important team meeting to attend. He introduced me and dashed off. No water, no coffee, no lunch, no help to move the table for my books to a better location. I felt like I'd been demoted from Broadway to the 'burbs overnight.

It's interesting that what really sticks with me about these two speaking engagements is not the size or response of the audience but the manner in which I was welcomed.

Now let me tell you about a library that does everything right. When it books an author for a program, the entire staff is informed. Bookmarks featuring the event are omnipresent at the circulation and reference desks and at self-checkout stations. Staff members tuck bookmarks into each stack of books that patrons bring to checkout, and they are prepared to chat enthusiastically about the event. A display featuring the author's works goes up well in advance of the event, and an article is written for the library newsletter. News releases, e-mail and Web notices are sent out in a timely manner.

All this is terrific, and good basic publicity protocol, but what makes this library special is that it goes the extra mile to make the author feel welcome. When I walked in with author Mark Salzman for a program, there was a student cellist entertaining the crowd in homage to Mark's background as a cellist and his book *The Soloist*.

A Maori storyteller from New Zealand was moved almost to tears when he walked in this library to find a display case showcasing all things New Zealand, including a photo of the Maori Queen. In the meeting room itself, a map of New Zealand had been tacked up, which the speaker happily used to show the audience where exactly he was from.

My mother always used to say (and probably yours did, too), "I'd rather have a little bit of quality than a whole lot of not so hot." She wasn't referring to author events, but the advice still works. Only do author events that you have the time, energy and staff to support really well. Don't get caught up in the program-a-week or program-a-month rat race and then be too frazzled to really honor your guest author.

Come on-a My House

If your author comes from out of town, she is probably going to need a place to stay. If you are working with an agent, he or she will make the arrangements. Publishers typically use the same hotel in a city for all of their visiting authors. If you are dealing directly with an author, it's nice to offer suggestions for convenient lodging in a variety of price ranges.

Here's a letter I wrote to one incoming author about six weeks before the program:

11 August 2006

Agatha Christie
10 Little Lane
Indianola, MO 67854

Dear Ms. Christie:

September is sneaking up on us and so is our "Women of Mystery" series. There's a lot of excited buzz amongst staff and patrons. We're all really looking forward to your arrival. As a matter of fact, we've already had a call from Alaska—someone had heard a rumor that you were coming and wanted confirmation so she could make plane reservations.

I promised I'd give you some suggestions for hotels. In thinking over your itinerary, I still think downtown Seattle is a good location. Our visiting authors have often stayed at the Westin (phone number), which is certainly pleasant enough in a tall, corncob tower sort of way. You mentioned the Alexis (phone number), another great place. My other suggestion would be The Inn at the Market (phone number) if you want to opt for a smaller hotel, like the Alexis, with a little local color. It is located right in the Pike Place Market with lots of easy access to good places to eat.

Unless you'd prefer to grab a cab from the airport, I'll plan on picking you up. As soon as I know your travel arrangements, I'll send you a detailed itinerary of the day. Our offices have recently moved, so I've enclosed a card with the new address and phone number.

Cordially,

Chapple Langemack
Reader's Services Coordinator

Like I said in Chapter 6, we pay our authors in one inclusive lump sum, so they are responsible for their own expenses. You can arrange for lodging in any way that you like as long as you, the author and the hotel are all clear on what's going on. We have been able to forge some relationships with individual hotels that will donate rooms for author visits if they aren't sold out. I've had widely varied success with this technique, but it certainly doesn't hurt to investigate. There may also be a lovely B&B in your area that would be a good option.

The most unique lodging I've ever had as a speaker was in a small town on the opposite side of the state, an eight-hour drive from my home. I'd been asked to do an all-day training for the staff. The host library had promised to arrange lodging for the night before the training. I rolled into town and checked in at the library and discovered that the lone motel in town was not deemed fit for me (it rented by the hour), so arrangements had been made at the local retirement home. The room turned out to be spacious, clean and comfortable (although I did wonder who died and left them the furniture). The rental, I discovered, was $35 a night. I left before the office opened the next day and, evidently, there had been a miscommunication between the home and the library. I received a call from the retirement facility, during the training, wondering why I'd skipped out without paying the tab. Ultimately the library folk got it all straightened out. I'll have to admit it was kind of exciting being a scofflaw for a few hours.

I would discourage you from offering a room in someone's home as a lodging option for an author. I arranged for an author for our foundation's big event one year, and a member of the foundation staff asked me if the author wouldn't like to stay in the home of one of the board members. This prospect made me a little nervous, even though it was a lovely waterfront home. I double-checked with the publisher's representative, and we agreed that it probably wasn't a good plan. (Actually, she said, "Nah. What if he wants to put his jockey shorts on his head and dance around?" How could I not agree?) It's best to allow an author a neutral space where he doesn't have to be "on." I spent quite a bit of time with this author, and even though he was warm and genial with everyone, he told me he always keeps the "Do Not Disturb" sign out on his hotel room so he wouldn't be bothered by housekeeping. A room in a private home, no matter how lovely, would probably not have been a good idea.

Some Digs!

Of course, there are homes and there are Homes. Authors who participate in the Des Moines Public Library's author program are invited to stay in the Governor's House. Jan Kaiser, who coordinates AviD (Authors Visiting in Des Moines), says that Iowa First Lady Christie Vilsack is a great friend to libraries and makes Terrace Hill, the Governor's Mansion, available for the event each year. The vivacious mystery author Lisa Scottoline was one such guest. "Picture Lisa," recounts Jan, "looking a little dubious as I'm driving up to the gate of this fabulous Victorian mansion. Lisa asked me, 'Does the Governor really live here?' I told her, 'Of course, it's the Governor's Mansion.' Lisa burst into gales of laughter, 'Oh my gosh, I thought it was just the name of a Bed & Breakfast!'"

Let's Eat!

Arranging meals for an author is another delicate dance. You really have to take your cue from the author. Some authors are very social, some are not. You just have to work around the schedule and their desires. If an author has an afternoon program, I check in with her to see if I should pick her up for lunch or if she'd rather lunch on her own. If I do have an author in tow for lunch, I try to find a spot that has at least a little local color. Some of my favorites in our neck of the woods are spots at the Pike Place Farmer's Market or at the restaurant overlooking Snoqualmie Falls. I once hosted an author who always ate sushi on Fridays, so we ate at a sushi bar on Lake Union. Try to have several options so you can accommodate the author's preference. Sometimes circumstances are beyond your control. I picked up an author at the airport once, and by the time the plane landed late and we got her luggage, we had very little time before her event. She was starving. We wound up at a fish taco place near the library. It was a pretty good fish taco place but…. Oh, well. We both got fed.

Now here's the uncomfortable part—and maybe you can figure out a system better than mine. We've paid the author a set fee that includes transportation, meals and lodging. And yet it seems churlish not to pick up the tab when you are hosting an author. Most of the time, it is my pleasure to take an author to lunch, even if it is on my own hook. I can't get reimbursed for my own meal nor for hers, though I'm sure that's what the author believes. I once had an author merrily invite several friends to dinner after an event. He was quite startled to find that they were expected to pay for their own meal. Your own funding situation may be different, but it's something to bear in mind. If you've got a partier on your hands who wants to have drinks at the hottest spot in town after his program, just don't forget to take your wallet along.

One of my favorite memories is when I was hosting the professional storyteller from New Zealand whom I mentioned earlier. This charming fellow not only insisted on paying for my meals, he would heap money into my hands and have me pay the check. Our money was too confusing, he told me cheerfully. It was all the same color, he couldn't figure it out.

Often time is tight, so I take a cue from professional media escorts and keep a basket of snacks and bottled water in the car. It's not the same as a meal, but in a pinch, at least you've got something. Here's a hint from experience: don't keep chocolate in your basket of snacks in the summertime.

Anatomy of a Snack Basket

- bottled water
- granola or protein bars
- packets of nuts
- fruit (organic is always a good idea)
- local gourmet potato chips
- local gourmet chocolate bar (in the winter)
- raisins and dried fruit
- crackers and cheese

Deirdre, a professional media escort gave me a great tip. She carries a small medicinal basket in her car as well with aspirin, band-aids, breath mints and eyedrops. When faced with an author trying to cope with laryngitis, Deirdre adds a thermos of hot water, tea and honey. Anything to try to make the author comfortable.

Grace Notes

I talked earlier about being able to tell your author about the event and the area. It's also a nice touch if you can gather together some local information. I would often need to take an author from one end of the county to the other. Sometimes I could see their eyes spin they were so disoriented. A map helps. I learned to give an author our library's flyer with all the branch libraries listed and shown on a map. A regular local map helps as well. It's always a good idea to have a list of local restaurants prepared. It doesn't have to be exhaustive, but a range of options is nice. If you expect that she will have some free time, you might want to include a list of local attractions.

If you want to make your author feel extra welcome, arrange for a gift basket in her room. Perhaps some fruit and some local treats. The most fun basket I've done was for someone whose taste I knew quite well. The basket was full of local gourmet chips, popcorn and microbrews with a few local chocolates to top it off. I don't know who enjoyed it more, me or the recipient!

So just use your best instincts to make your author feel welcome and you'll be a great host.

10

The Main Event

So now it's showtime. You've planned and communicated and confirmed, and the day of your program has finally arrived. You've checked and prepared the room, and you need only for the author to appear and the audience to show up.

Awaiting the Author

If a professional media escort is accompanying your author, the escort will probably call you in the morning or the day before to let you know that the author is in town and confirm (once again) the event and make sure her directions are correct. At that time, she'll let you know when to expect the author to arrive. Usually they'll arrive fifteen minutes before the start of the event.

Arrival time can be a real source of tension between the programmer and the author. You as the event giver really want to know your ducks are in a row and that your program is really on. You never really feel sure that you won't have to break out your tap shoes until you see the whites of your author's eyes. On the other hand, some authors really hate hanging out before an event. One gentleman asked me to drive around a little bit so we wouldn't arrive so early. The hosts wanted him to be there forty-five minutes before. Five minutes was plenty for him. One poet, a former Poet Laureate, didn't mind arriving early but lamented that people wouldn't talk to him. Everyone thought he was preparing, thinking deep poetical thoughts and shouldn't be disturbed.

One time I arrived with an author ten minutes late to an event. It's not because the author was reticent, I just couldn't find a parking place. The library was packed with people eagerly waiting to hear the author, and we drove around and around looking for a place to park. That's when I learned to set aside a parking place for the author.

There is also the issue of tardy authors, which is a tricky issue if you are the escort. Some authors just live a little closer to the edge, timewise, than I am comfortable with. It's not always a blatant disregard for time; sometimes it's an unexpected phone call or inspiration. Unless you're escorting an author over the course of several days, you have no way of knowing that and adjusting your pickup time accordingly. When I establish a pickup time, I generally leave a little cushion, just because traffic is so unpredictable around here. So far, I've never been kept waiting more than ten or fifteen minutes, but those can be some long minutes.

I asked a professional media escort how she dealt with tardy authors. She started by saying that it's a pretty rare occurrence. Then she told me that when she arrives at the appointed time, she has the hotel desk ring the room to let the author know that she's there. If the author isn't down in five minutes, she has them ring him again at ten minutes. At fifteen minutes, she has them ring him again and then calls the program planner (or newsroom) and tells them she's waiting on the author, that he's been dinged three times. This means it's important for you as the event planner to have a phone on your person. You don't want to be racing back to your cubicle to see if the media escort has phoned with an update.

However (and whenever) your author arrives, you'll want to have someone stationed near the door to greet him and take him to wherever it is you want him to wait—the hallway, an office, the green room, or just the back of the auditorium. It's good manners to let your author know that the bookseller has arrived and is set up and offer your impressions of the crowd: "I recognize a lot of ladies from book clubs here tonight, but I did see that two men snuck in. We set up 200 chairs and they are all full."

Now is the time to confirm (again) the length of his talk and that there will be a Q&A session. Let him know if there are time constraints: "The library closes at nine." Find out how much time and crowd management he wants from you. Some authors are old pros and have no problems cutting off questions when it's time. Some will ask you to give a high sign at a certain point so they know how much time they have left. Some authors feel obliged to stay and answer every last question, bless them. That's a good thing for you to know in advance. You can feel pretty silly looming and giving high signs to which the author has no intention of paying any heed.

As I Was Saying ...

Sometimes we do our best to meet an author's expectations and are, well, surprised. When Larry King visited Davis County Library, he let Judy know in no uncertain terms that he was only going to hang around for a few minutes; he had other things to do. Judy gulped and agreed that that was just fine. He did an interview before the program, and then Judy explained the format: speak for a few minutes; take questions from the audience and then a book signing. Larry King replied, "Well, I'm just not gonna be here that long." Once again, Judy agreed, "That's just fine, Mr. King," thinking she'd just have to go with the flow. Once he got to the podium and started speaking, Judy relates, "It was like someone turned him on. He's magic. And then the audience starts asking questions, and I'm looking at my watch thinking he wants out of here, I know he does." So Judy caught his eye and say, "Mr. King, I know you have another engagement, so when you need to shut this down I would like you to leave a few minutes for book signings," and he said, "I don't need to be anywhere!" The man who could only stay for a few minutes stayed for nearly an hour and a half.

Let your author know that there is water at the podium and where he'll go to sign books. See if there's anything else that he or the escort needs. You don't need to be obsequious, just pleasant. I knew I'd overdone it one time. We had a very big-name author with an equally big following in the Northwest and a very full house, close to 500 people. We were so pleased to have him there, and I was psyched. He had had a number of requirements and even came with bodyguard in tow. When I asked him if there was anything else he needed, this wag cocked an eyebrow at me and said, "A map of Madagascar, perhaps?" Oh, well.

Allow Me to Introduce

You've decided in advance who will introduce the author, be it you or the chairman of the library board or the mayor or whoever. If it's not you, you'll probably want to provide the introducer with a few key biographical facts and a guideline as to how long they should speak. This is also the time you let the audience know the drill: "Mr. Proust will take questions after his remarks and will be signing books in the lobby after the program. You may have noticed as you came in that our local independent bookseller has books for sale near the entrance."

Please, please, please make your introduction brief. Everyone knows who they came to hear, for Pete's sake, or they wouldn't be there. The job of the introduction is to let people know they are in the right place (the flight to Milwaukee and not to Atlanta), give them time to settle in, take care of any housekeeping matters and to make the presenter feel welcome and appreciated. This should take two or three minutes, tops. Remember all those excruciating introductions you've sat through. Don't do that! I once had a professor in library school who was a very personable fellow and a great storyteller. Unfortunately, when he introduced a speaker he became dry as dust and encyclopedic to boot. You could judge the importance of the occasion or the speaker by the length of the introduction. I timed him out at twenty minutes once at a Very Important National Lecture. Ye Gads! Don't make your introduction an endurance test.

On another occasion, I escorted an author, a noted journalist, to an event at a neighboring library. He was introduced by the editor of the regional newspaper that was cosponsoring the event. The editor was quite struck by the parallels between his own life and that of the speaker. He was so entranced by them he went on about it at great length. From journalism school on, each remarkable resemblance was noted. Finally the author, tired of waiting behind the stage curtain stuck a hand out and waved. Then he stuck a foot out. Then he stuck a hand and foot out. The audience was mightily entertained. The editor was not. Rather than taking the hint and cutting to the chase, he chastised the guest speaker and continued on with his prepared remarks. Sheesh. Luckily the author was more than up to the task of regaining the audience that the editor had put to sleep, but his remarks in the car later were less than kind.

So when you're introducing a speaker, make it personal if you can, be warm, be flattering, be brief. Stay at the podium until the author arrives there, shake hands and exit stage right (or left as the case may be).

We hosted Jayne Ann Krentz the other night, and I thought our programming librarian, Lisa, hit just the right note with this:

"Welcome to our program this evening. I'd like to thank the Bellevue Friends of the Library for their continuing support of our author programs. Tonight we are pleased to welcome best-selling author Jayne Ann Krentz.

"Consider this for a moment—Jayne Ann Krentz has written more than 140 books under six different names. She sets her stories in the past, present and future, in locations as near as Seattle and as far away as another solar system. What do they have in common? In her own words, 'romance, suspense, a lot of family stuff, some humor and a psychic twist.' Oh, and the girl always gets the guy in the end. What more could you want?

"Please welcome Jayne Ann Krentz."

One clever author sends out his own introduction and it's printed out in extra large type so that a person can easily read it at the podium. It looks like this:

INTRODUCTION SHEET

ERNEST HEMINGWAY ...

WRITER, WAR CORRESPONDENT, AMBULANCE DRIVER

HE WRITES ...

A WEEKLY COLUMN ON THE ART OF BULLFIGHTING WHICH IS THE MOST WIDELY SYNDICATED SPORTS COLUMN IN AMERICA

HE HOSTS ...

A RADIO SHOW ON THE JOYS OF FISHING ALONE

HE IS ...

THE AUTHOR OF TWELVE BEST SELLERS INCLUDING ISLANDS IN THE STREAM AND A MOVEABLE FEAST

HE HAS ...

APPEARED ON JOHNNY CARSON AND THE DAILY SHOW WITH JON STEWART

When the speaker has concluded, it's important to reappear at the podium. This is a visual clue that the event (or at least that portion of it) is over. Thank the speaker, thank the audience for coming and give the audience any necessary marching orders. "Ms. Austen will be signing her books at this table in just a few moments. Please help yourself to refreshments."

Q&A

The question-and-answer period is often the real guts of an author event. Many savvy authors give the briefest of presentations then turn it over to Q&A and, essentially, have a conversation with the audience. That's what turns a passive event into an interactive event and really engages those attending. (I do have a writer friend who heartily disagrees: "I want to hear the author read!" she tells me plaintively.) Most authors have no trouble negotiating Q&A, although some may need help cutting off questions. If you're expecting a really big crowd or if you have a darkened hall, you may wish to have the audience write their questions down to be collected and asked by a moderator. This allows you much more control over the Q&A session. You can eliminate redundant questions (plus the long-winded questioner) and opt for the freshest, most interesting questions in your batch.

We chose this technique when hosting Tom Robbins talking about his book *Villa Incognito*. Here are some of the questions we collected. You can draw your own conclusions about which questions we asked.

- What can I do tomorrow to thwart our facist government?
- Being that eroticism is such an oddball focus in so much of what you write, what for you would be a truly erotic experience?
- When did you start writing stories?
- Exaggerated genitalia? OK, then. 'Splain some of inspiration? Childhood?
- What was the cause of the biggest laugh you ever had? What makes you laugh?
- Are you married?
- Which one of your books is your favorite?
- How much pot did you smoke while writing your books?
- Which authors do you read over and over or feel inspired by and why?

- Have you traveled in the countries you write about? (Not armchair travel, virtual travel or out-of-body travel.)
- Do you enjoy speaking in front of people?
- I lost my phone number, can I have yours?
- Have you been to Nepal?
- Do you think you are a good writer? How much do you struggle with it?
- Are you single?
- Do you continue to write in the style you do and about the same subjects because it has been successful and you want to continue making money, or do you still actually enjoy writing the way you do?
- Who is your favorite rock band?
- What author had the most impact on your writing career? And what shoe size do you wear?
- How do you walk the line between off-the-wall storytelling and crass reader alienation? Do you have a line?
- What are you eating? Are you going to finish it?
- You always have very strong female protagonists. Who or what are your inspirations for these characters?
- When did you first feel your readers were listening, and how did it influence your writing?
- What is the best thing about being a writer? What is the worst thing about being a writer?
- Approximately what proportion of the ideas espoused in your books are ideas that you are exploring to those which you actually hold truck with?
- Which do you think came first, the chicken or the egg?
- What gave you the idea to create characters out of inanimate objects in *Skinny Legs and All?*
- What does it feel like when you finish a book?
- Do you like your readers? Do you think people take what you write differently than you intend? Do you cave?
- Does making money by writing books—the business of writing—get in the way of your creativity?
- Why did the chicken cross the road really?

- Where's the other pyramid on a pack of camels? I can't find the damn thing!
- Do you have a good relationship with your father?
- If you woke up in Attorney General John Ashcroft's body, which civil liberty would you suspend next?
- Are you happy? Elaborate.
- Describe yourself, if you will, as ingredients of a tasty meal.
- What is the most bizarre piece of fan mail you ever received?
- Is your writing done in fits and spurts or do you work with discipline?

Crowd Control

I don't know about you, but I spend most of my time worrying about getting a respectable number of people to show up to an event. How to manage the crowd that you get, and what to do about a large or overflow crowd, bear careful consideration as well.

Depending on the size of your hall and the audience you expect, it's a good idea to have "ushers." Even for events where we only expect fifty to seventy-five people, it's nice to have two or three staff members or volunteers on hand. For big events, I like to have six or eight. I never do assigned seating, so the ushers don't really "ush." They greet and answer questions, guide people to the auditorium and the restrooms and the drinking fountain. They tell them how long the program is, if the author will sign books, where the books can be purchased, who the bookseller is, and who is sponsoring the program. You'd be surprised at how many questions people have and how glad they are to have an easily identifiable body to ask.

To Ticket or Not to Ticket

There are two schools of thought when it comes to ticketing an event. You might think that the way to get the precise number of people you want at an event is to hand out a precise number of tickets. Well, I'm sorry to dash your dreams here darlin', but it just ain't necessarily so. I became a ticket unbeliever back in the days when I had to manage registration for preschool storytime. It quickly became clear to me that the people who sign up for an event don't necessarily feel obliged to show up. Likewise, the people who don't register in advance feel perfectly free to drop in. So what, I ask you, is the point? I quickly tired of verbally grappling with parents over whether they could bring their three-year-old to storytime. I became a firm believer in first come, first served, and when there's no more room, better luck next time. It sounds coldhearted, I know, but I'm convinced it's the only way to keep your sanity, especially when you're dealing with free programs. Laura Dudnik, programmer at the Evanston Public Library in Illinois, has had similar experiences. "We tried required registration for our events mainly because it would be nice to know how many chairs to set up and to be able to tell the publisher how many people to expect. However, our patrons just flat out refused to do it, so we gave up the idea."

Laura and I aren't the only ones who came to this conclusion. Nextbook is a nonprofit organization dedicated to the promotion of Jewish culture and literature. In their maiden voyage in Seattle, they linked up with the local libraries. The Nextbook fellow had an office at King County Library System's Service Center and did some of her programming in King County Library System and Seattle Public Libraries. Because the library was a sponsoring organization, the agreement was not to charge for programming. Instead tickets were made available by request. Guess what? Up to 80 percent of those holding tickets never showed up to the program. Finally, frustrated to the core, the Nextbook operation moved to the University of Washington where they could charge for tickets. Sometimes, we in the free public library lament that folks just don't value what they get for free. We'll see if this proves to be the case for Nextbook.

Now, just as I was settling down comfortably in my "no tickets!" scrooge mode, I talked to Judy about tickets. She has a 250-seat auditorium and hosts some of the biggest names around. I asked her what she did about crowd control. "Oh, we issue tickets," she said blithely. But Judy, I said, what do you do about no-shows? "The tickets are only good until fifteen minutes before the program. If you're not in your seat by then, we give it to someone else." Imagine the sound of me smiting my forehead. Judy went on to tell me exactly how it works:

Tickets are issued at a certain time on a certain day at one location. Each ticket comes with a verbal warning about the fifteen-minute rule plus a cautionary flyer about the fifteen-minute rule. Plus the ticket clearly says, "Doors open at 6:30 P.M. This ticket reserves one seat only until 6:45 P.M., after which time non–ticket holders will be seated."

Now I know that Judy's events attract people from all over. I wondered what people from long distances did to procure a ticket. "Sometimes they drive in to get them. Sometimes they have friends or relatives who pick them up for them." Judy also told me that there is a limit of two tickets per person. I wondered how they kept track. So I asked what prevented someone from coming back later on, or the next day and getting more tickets. I could hear Judy smiling over the phone when she said, "Oh, they are all given out in the first ten minutes. We don't have to worry about *later*."

People who aren't lucky enough to get tickets are also advised of the fifteen-minute rule. They get a flyer that says:

IF YOU DID NOT GET TICKETS TO TERI GARR ...

Keep in mind that standby seating is often available, but not guaranteed, the night of the program. The line for standby seating forms quickly and operates on a first-come, first-served basis.

If you are unable to get seats for the program, you can still meet Ms. Garr and have your books signed as the auditorium begins to empty. We estimate the book signing will begin at about 7:45 P.M.

If you choose to operate by the first-come, first-served theory, you need to warn people in advance and you need to set limits. All of my flyers and advertising for author events have this statement: "This program is free and open to the public. Seating is limited. First come, first served."

Having warned people, you then need to be prepared to turn them away should you have a huge crowd. If you don't do it, the fire department most certainly will. They take seating limitations very seriously. You also need to be firm about sitting or standing in inappropriate places. Don't be afraid to identify empty seats from the podium and herd standees into them. I guess it's commitment-phobia—no one wants to sit in front or in the middle of a row. They'd rather hang out standing at the back of the room. They must think if it's no good, they can bolt without anyone noticing.

At one recent program, a mom and two young sons arrived twenty minutes late. "Oh!" she exclaimed, quite surprised, "Has it already started?" Grrrrr. Yes, as a matter of fact it had, and the room was packed. Her solution was to stand in the doorway with the children. It was the only doorway to the room. She was not all that pleased when I told her, quite nicely, that she either needed to go in and find a seat or leave. It actually reminded me of holding the door for my cat, Jemimah, who like all cats, takes her own sweet time deciding whether the outdoors really beckons or not. The battle cry at our front door is, "Commit, Jemimah! Commit!"

Now if you charge for tickets to your events, all this is beside the point. You have so many seats, you sell so many tickets. Whether people actually come or not ceases to be a concern. If you take reservations for tickets without payment, then you're back on the fire again. How long will you hold them? Will you release them before curtain? If so, how long before? It just gets more and more complicated. Whether you charge or not, my advice is to adopt a simple policy and stick to it.

Block and Tackle

The other tricky thing about crowds and author events is maintaining breathing space for your author. We welcomed Nikki Giovanni one year, who drew a tremendous crowd in a relatively small space. We had the bright idea of putting the bookseller and signing table out in the foyer to save space in the room itself. The only problem with that was it left me with the task of getting Ms. Giovanni from the podium through the crowd, out the door and to the signing table. I didn't realize it was going to be a problem until the audience began to crowd around Ms. Giovanni right after her remarks. She's not a very big person and is extremely gracious. I was a little concerned she would get trampled … and never get to the signing table. Finally I flung out my elbows and apologies and bulldozed a path toward the signing table. That was a big lesson for me. Now I think very hard about the placement of the signing table and the path to get to it. I've also learned to instruct the audience to queue in a certain place. Most of the time people will do what you want, if you tell them what it is.

Lines and Signing

Have your ushers be very clear about where the line for the book sales is and where the line for the signing is, if they are two different lines. If it's a big crowd and a long line, have the ushers work the line. Have them hand out Post-It notes and pencils so that people can write down the inscription they want on their book. Have them joke and chat with the folks in the line. Do a little market research about how people found out about the program. Thank them frequently for their patience. Judy has been known to circulate through the line with cookies.

If there are rules about signing, have the ushers let attendees know. Sometimes authors will only sign, they won't personalize books. Prolific authors will sometimes have a limit on the number of books they'll sign. This is a very good thing to find out in advance from the publicist so that you can put it on your flyer and announce it from the podium. I've often found, however, that these sorts of restrictions only pop up at the moment, so use your ushers to let people know so they don't stand in line for something they are not going to get.

If you have to, God forbid, cut off a line, do it as soon as you know. The vast majority of the authors we've hosted have been as gracious as they could possibly be and have signed every last book requested of them—and that includes stock signing for the book store. Tom Robbins, bless his heart, signed for two hours. And people waited for two hours. Patiently and politely. Only once have I had an author falter at a signing. She is a prolific author and had lots to sign. About six people were still waiting, when she began to show fatigue and say she didn't think she could go on. I encouraged her mightily and did everything I could think of short of mopping her brow and fanning her with feathers. She did make it through the final few people, but it felt touch and go there for a while.

After an author is done signing for the public, the bookseller may ask if she will sign stock—unsold books that the bookseller will be able to offer at her store. This is pretty standard practice and doesn't require anything from you. The bookseller will generally do the asking, and I've yet to hear an author refuse.

Closing Out the Event

When all the chores are taken care of, thank the author again for her visit. If you want her to come back, say so: "Please remember us when your next book comes out." When I was doing author events for all of King County Library System, it was fun to be able to say, "Remember, I have forty-two other venues. We'd be glad to have you back."

If money changes hands, now is the time to pass the check over discreetly in an envelope. Now is also a good time to ask the author for a mailing address if you don't already have it, so that you can send a thank you note. I've always felt funny about just asking for an author's address, and then Judy gave me a good tip. "We make packets of the publicity the program received for the author and for the publicist. I always ask the author if they'd like for me to send them the clippings. They almost always do … and, of course, I guard the address with my life."

Make yourself available to the audience members as they are leaving so they can have a word with you if they care to. Have your ushers collect the evaluations or make sure there is a well-marked spot where evaluations go.

And that's it. Say goodnight to your audience as they leave. Bid your author adieu. Clean up the venue, and collect what you'll need for your own evaluation and follow-up. Pat yourself on the back; you've had a successful author event.

If It Can Go Wrong, It Might

Ninety-nine percent of the time, your author event will go smoothly, but there may be an occasion where things don't go quite as planned. Is there anything you can do to save the day?

The largest percentage of things that might go awry can be headed off by good advance planning. Double- and triple-checking on the date with the author and publicist, making sure the escort or limo driver knows exactly where the venue is and the time of the event, having a backup computer for a PowerPoint presentation—all these things are good insurance for a trouble-free event. If despite your best efforts, something goes wrong, you need to smile, think fast and roll with it.

Where Oh Where?

Every program planner's worst nightmare is that the author just plain doesn't show up—or cancels at the last minute. If you have advance notice, you can do your best to get the word out via the media. If you don't, you don't have many options other than greeting the audience and giving them the news. Put a sandwich board in front of your building if you can, especially if parking is hard to come by. That will save someone from wrestling for a parking place and coming into the building only to find the program has been cancelled. Put a sign on the door, certainly, but don't just do that. Station someone at the door to tell people personally and apologize. Even though it's not your fault, you must empathize with the folks who made an effort to come to the event. One of my enterprising programming librarians stood at the door to the meeting room with a basket of chocolate to offer to the disappointed attendees. One bookseller still shudders when she recounts having to apologize individually to the 900 people who showed up to hear a well-known writer. In this case, the bookstore involved also offered refunds to all those who had purchased a book in anticipation of having it signed by the author.

Resist the temptation to reveal unflattering details or trash the author. You might not be particularly happy that the author blew you off to appear on *Oprah,* but really, who can blame him? Limit yourself to saying something unexpected came up or that the author had a personal emergency. Content yourself with the fact that you did say "author events are subject to change at the last minute" on all of your publicity. If you're able to reschedule prior to the cancelled event, have flyers with the new date handy. Otherwise, take phone numbers and e-mail addresses and promise to notify folks if you are able to reschedule.

What Did You Say Your Name Was?

The event planner's second biggest nightmare is if the presenter shows up, um, impaired. Or perhaps just naturally a little more "out there" than you expected. This is a situation that you need to play by ear. One organizer told me she had a celebrity speaker show up drunk and with a homeless person in tow. Luckily, the speaker was able to present without a problem, so she made his new friend comfortable and went on with the show.

Remember that the crowd that shows up for a particular person may be expecting a particular kind of behavior even though it might not be what you, the event planner, thought you had signed on for. One bookseller reports that she was greatly taken aback when an author began to throw plastic penises out to the crowd. The crowd, however, took it in stride and seemed very happy with the state of affairs. The show went on. Another author boasts that no reading is a success unless someone in the audience faints or throws up, and that often happens. I can only hope that I do my homework well enough to never book this particular author.

Sometimes—rarely, but sometimes—things will go out of bounds and you must intercede. When a young actor/author began making out with young women in the signing line, one bookseller recalled her own teenaged children. "I told him to stop that! And settled him down to sign books." Another author, a scientist, was slated to talk about dolphins and whales but instead began a religious rant. The event planner read the unease in the crowd and stopped the presenter with, "I'm sorry, there must have been some confusion about the topic today." She then apologized to the audience and escorted the author to his car. "I'm not sure what happened," she reports, "I think the man may have had a psychotic break."

Happy Endings

Remember that instances such as these are few and far between. If you've planned and prepared well, the vast majority of your events will go just as you have planned and be enormously rewarding for you, the author and your audience.

11

The Really Big Do

If everyday author events are all about planning, then big author events are all about planning big time. Doing a fundraising dinner or a book festival is like writing a book instead of an essay. There are more components to keep in your head, and it takes longer to do. Actually, there's more of everything. You need more lead time to plan, there are more logistical details (seating, food, decoration), there may be more venues, more partner and sponsor agencies and there are almost always more people involved (guests, committee and volunteers).

You really have to know what you're about with these kinds of functions or you'll get lost in the morass of detail midway through. All the festival planners I've chatted with break planning down into assigning functional responsibilities and establishing timelines. But first, of course, you need to establish the basics.

Why a Big Do?

Fairs and festivals have goals just like regular programs do. While regular programs may contribute to the overall aims of the library or agency, a big do generally has a really specific raison d'etre. There may be a primary and secondary goal. King County Library System Foundation's Literary Lions dinner honors someone in the community who has made a great contribution to the cause of literary. It's also a way to educate and enlist the support of foundation donors for ongoing programs. I mentioned in an earlier chapter that part of the purpose of Charlotte's literary festival, Novello, was to make a big splash for the library. A secondary purpose for the library and the newspaper sponsors was to make something exciting happen in downtown Charlotte. For Martin County Library, Bookmania! showed off its new buildings in a big way.

The folks at Des Moines Public Library crafted goals and guidelines for their big literary event Authors Visiting in Des Moines (AViD), and I think they are pretty good ones:

Des Moines Public Library AViD Author Series Guidelines

Purpose—a celebration of books, authors, and the joy of reading. Established in 2001 as an outreach effort of the Des Moines Public Library and funded by donations to its foundation, the author series presents writers who are outstanding speakers with a variety of subjects and viewpoints to stimulate, enlighten, and entertain the community of Des Moines.

Held annually in the spring, this event will highlight the lifelong learning opportunities offered by the library. Additional fundraising events may be planned in conjunction with the author visits such as writing workshops, book signings and receptions, but the opportunity to listen to well-recognized authors will be free and open to the general public. This event will demonstrate how a library can touch the hearts and minds of its customers.

Goals

- Showcase authors of both national and regional stature.
- Present authors of diverse cultural backgrounds.
- Provide one or more free author programs open to the public.
- Offer other workshops or fundraisers in conjunction with author visits.
- Offer outreach programs at schools or other locations.
- Showcase additional free programming such as book discussion groups, book signings and workshops conjunction with the author programs.
- Develop partnerships with other agencies and businesses in support of books and reading.
- Help the library attract and reach new customers, thereby increasing library usage.

- Establish pride in the library and the community.
- Give an opportunity for increased library collaboration with corporate and nonprofit communities.
- Help to establish the library as a cultural center in Des Moines.
- Show that the library is a forum for the reader, the writer and the listener.

Just like smaller-scale events, once you have your goal, all other decisions spring from there—theme, time of year, type of venue, audience base, potential sponsors, talent, décor and food. It's at this point that any event starts sorting itself out by function.

Who Does What?

For several years, King County Library System produced Storyfest, an international storytelling festival. The goal of Storyfest was to let people of different cultures know they had a home in the library. For three days, storytellers from around the world converged to entertain children, teens, adults and seniors. On the first day, storytellers were taken out to branch libraries, senior centers and day camps to extend the venue and create excitement for the event. On the second and third days, storytellers rotated through five venues in and around a large library, each for a designated age group. Three of the venues were tents in the park next to the library. The planners of Storyfest knew they wanted an outdoor festival, which meant taking the weather into consideration. They had to figure out what to do if it rained (which it did by the bucketful one year) and what to do if it got terribly hot (which it does occasionally do in Seattle). It was a really big do.

Le Corbusier was right, God truly is in the detail with these sorts of events. You must be a listmaker extraordinaire to keep track of everything. And dare I say it? No one does a festival by herself. Begin to think of your event in terms of functions to be assigned (or volunteered for) so that everyone has a clear idea of what is in her area of responsibility.

Divide and Conquer

Sally Porter, former Youth Services Coordinator for KCLS, ramrodded Storyfest for several years. She breaks down responsibilities for this kind of event into four major categories. Each category has a project manager who plans the details ahead of time and is on-site during the event armed with a walkie-talkie for instant communication. Each project manager reports to the festival supervisor who keeps, or attempts to keep, everything on track.

Talent

The person in charge of talent is the person who is the contact for the performers, be they authors or storytellers. She arranges for the booking, contracts, housing, and schedules and keeps the performers apprised of ongoing plans on a regular basis. She gets to deal with the Immigration and Naturalization Service if any of the performers require a visa to get into the country. This is the person who makes sure each performer is met at the airport and taken to their lodging. (In the case of Storyfest, all of the storytellers were lodged in a motel close to the main venue. We got a deal on multiple rooms and the storytellers loved being around one another.) This is the person who arranged for escorts if storytellers went out into the satellite venues.

During the festival, this person is the essential contact for all of the performers. She will maintain a "green room" for their comfort and see that they had everything they need. She also makes sure each performer shows up for his appointed appearance.

Virginia Stanley at HarperCollins calls this whole business "author care," and while it's important for any author event, it's critical for large-scale programs. No one performer is the star attraction, and yet you want all authors involved to feel like they are an especially honored guest.

Judi Snyder feels that her volunteer author escorts are the key. "We hold a fun cocktail party the evening before Bookmania! Our escorts bring the authors to the party from their hotels and see that they are wined and dined and introduced. That way, even if they are shy, the escorts see that they have a good time." Claire Wilkinson provides Literary Lions authors with a ribbon, a sash, a corsage or boutonniere so that they are easily identifiable by other guests. She recommends that you make sure to greet your guest authors and introduce them to library board members or staff so that they have someone to talk to.

Claire also suggests, "If space allows, create some poster-size displays with author photos, biographies and book lists. Or create a looping video with author photos, etc. to give guests an opportunity to learn more about the authors. After mingling and before the program begins, briefly introduce authors to the crowd.

"During the event, try to circulate and chat with your authors and introduce them to guests with whom they might share interests. Make an effort to say goodbye to each author at the end of the event. After the event, send a short thank-you card and perhaps a small gift such as a library mug or T-shirt or library-themed notecards."

Visa, Please

Dealing with perfomers from around the world has an interesting wrinkle. It's called the Immigration and Naturalization Service (INS). Because the main goal of Storyfest was to showcase world cultures, festival organizers brought in storytellers from around the world, which meant dealing with INS. "Dealing with the INS adds six months to your planning process right off the bat," says festival organizer Sally Porter. "Our event took place in August, but the INS wouldn't consider visa applications before the first of the year. It invariably took a year or more for the visas to be processed so we'd end up getting visas for a performer six months after the event. Talk about Catch-22. And this was before September 11!" Her advice to others who want to bring in international talent? "Be smart like the International Children's Festival and have some really sharp immigration attorneys on your board of directors."

Transportation

This person coordinates transportation for the audience. If you're having an event that you expect to draw several thousand people and you have parking for several hundred, you need to coordinate off-site parking and shuttles. This person finds available parking lots to use for the event. In our case, it was nearby churches. She procures the use of shuttle buses, finds drivers for them and figures out how to get them back to their original home in a timely manner. She sets up a schedule of drivers and greeters at the off-site parking to let audience members know where to go and what to expect.

Here's the kind of detail that drives you nuts. You want children to come to this event, right? And yet, you can't bus young children in from off-site parking because you'd need carseats for every child. So you need to arrange for special on-site parking for kids. Which brings us to …

Parking

This is the person who gets to prepare a traffic plan and submit it to the city should the municipality require it. He will also recruit the volunteers to guide cars and redirect people to off-site parking when appropriate. He'll need to figure out on-site parking for the handicapped, those with special needs, the elderly and those pesky carseat kids. He'll need to know where the shuttle buses will load and unload and where emergency vehicles will be able to park, if needed.

Facilities

This person manages everything to do with the venues. She gets to rent the tents and the sound equipment and the porta-potties and make sure that everything is clean and secure over the course of the festival. She arranges for extra janitorial service for inside venues and for timely garbage pickup inside and outside. She makes sure the restrooms are clean and that there's enough toilet paper. I don't know how much toilet paper 5,000 people are likely to use, but this person gets to figure that out. She also needs to know what to do in case of power outages, blown fuses and random door or fire alarms. She'll have the proper forms ready in case there's an accident or injury on-site. She'll hire extra security if that's required and make sure the venue is cleaned up after the event.

Volunteers

Any really big event typically uses huge numbers of volunteers. Volunteers help manage the performers, the traffic, the venue, the crowd and just about everything else. Volunteers escort the performers and introduce them to the audience. They also keep the performers on time. Volunteers keep the green room stocked with food and drink for the performers and answer questions from the public. All these volunteers needs a coordinator who will recruit and train them and see to their needs. He needs to make sure that the volunteers are trained and that they clearly understand their job descriptions. He must provide any tools or assistance needed by the volunteers, be it extension cords or scripts. If the volunteers get T-shirts, this is the guy who makes sure each volunteer gets one. He will also make sure there is a relaxation room set up for the volunteers to rest, refresh and have a snack.

General Oversight

This is the commander in chief. She'll worry about budget and insurance and keep her eye on the intent of the event. If there are sponsors for the event, this is the person who keeps them in the loop. All of the project managers will report to her, during the planning and during the event itself. She'll have a list of who is doing what and make decisions when the unexpected crops up. She'll bring the project managers together after the event to decide what went right and what needs to be improved for the next year.

So there you have a general look at what needs to go of for a big event or festival. It's a matter of thinking through all the logistics, working with a team and making lots and lots and lots of lists and lots and lots of timelines. Let's take a look at those next.

Hey Kids, What Time Is It?

For really big events, there are several kinds of timelines, from broad strokes outlining what needs to be done each month to minute-by-minute accounts of what happens on the day(s) of the event.

Here's one yearly festival's broad outline of the planning process. You'll see that it begins for the following year before the current year's event has happened and ends not with but after the event for evaluation and follow-up.

Reading Festival

Sample Timeline

18 Months before Festival

☐ Start discussing festival components, speakers for following year
☐ Planning team in place, meeting every six weeks
☐ Determine budget

12 Months before Festival

☐ Evaluate current year, make notes for following year
☐ Unspecific schedule in place
☐ Speakers signed
☐ Partners on board
☐ Begin recruiting sponsors and volunteers
☐ Begin contacting vendors

6 Months before Festival

☐ Finalize schedule
☐ Start media campaign
☐ Start ticket sales
☐ Communicate with other staff
☐ Write and review detailed to-do list

3 Months before Festival

☐ Team starts to meet every other week
☐ Start special promotions, if needed
☐ Start minute-by-minute schedule

1 Month before Festival

☐ Team starts to meet every week
☐ Determine potential "trouble spots"
☐ Confirm details with all vendors (caterers, AV providers, venues, etc.)

1 Week before Festival

☐ Have final team meeting, review minute-by-minute schedule
☐ Review timelines, schedules, to-do lists: finalize all details
☐ Continue troubleshooting

Festival Week

☐ Keep minute-by-minute at all times
☐ Motivate staff, reward efforts
☐ Enjoy the event!

1 Week after Festival

☐ Thank everyone involved (team members, other staff, speakers, etc.)
☐ Organize records for easy reference
☐ Evaluate

As the event draws nearer, timelines get much more specific. Claire does yeoman work each year for the KCLS Foundation's splashy dinner, Literary Lions. This event has several challenges. First of all, it has not one author, but twenty. There is a keynote speaker and authors from the area, so no matter what table you sit at, you are in the company of an author. Here's a sample timeline that Claire uses starting six or seven months out from the event.

2000 Literary Lions—Task List			
Task	**Time Frame**	**Point Person**	
Sponsors solicited	Sep–Dec	Claire	Pending
Sponsor packets sent (guest list form, author bios, invoice)	Feb	Claire	
Authors invited	Sep–Dec	Claire	Done
Speaker invited—Lisa Scottoline	Sep–Dec	Jeanne	Done
Emcee invited—Lowell Deo	Sep–Dec	Claire	Done
Literary Lions Awards			
Nominations solicited	Nov–Dec	Claire	Done
Review committee solicited	Dec–Jan		Done
Meeting scheduled, nominations reviewed	Dec–Jan	Claire	Done
Notification to winners	Jan		Done
News release written and sent	Jan		
Lion statues purchased	Dec–Jan	Claire	Done
Lion statues engraved	Feb		
Review committee thanked	Jan	Claire	

Bellevue Regional Library			
Meet with BRL staff	Jan–Feb	Committee	Pending
Go over floor plan (podium, table, bar, book sale placement)	Jan–Feb	Committee	Pending
Review A/V needs	Jan–Feb	Committee	Pending
Table assignments/seating	Jan–Feb	Committee	Pending
Day-of setup	Mar		Pending
Cleanup	Mar		Pending
Catering		Berta	
Ask for proposals	Oct–Nov	Berta	Done
Review proposals	Oct–Nov	Berta	Done
Select caterer	Oct–Nov	Berta	Done
Determine menu	Oct–Nov	Berta	Done
Food and Beverage			
Solicit/follow up See's	Nov–Dec	Claire	Yes
Solicit/follow up Seattle Chocolates	Nov–Dec	Claire	Yes
Solicit/follow up Fran's	Nov–Dec	Claire	No
Solicit/follow up Dilettante	Nov–Dec	Claire	Pending
Solicit/follow up Godiva	Nov–Dec	Claire	Pending
Solicit/follow up Chateau St. Michelle	Nov–Dec	Claire	No
Solicit/follow up Columbia	Nov–Dec	Julia	Emp. Discount
Solicit/follow up Western Beverage	Nov–Dec	Claire	Yes
Obtain liquor license	Mar	Berta	
Get system approval to serve alcohol	Feb	Jeanne	Done
Decorations and Favors			
Solicit/follow up Molbak's	November	Claire	Done
Author favors			
KCLS mugs?	Feb	Claire	
Chocolates?	Feb	Claire	
Solicit/follow up Third Place/ Elliott Bay	Dec–Jan	Claire	Done
Solicit/folow up Tully's	Dec–Jan	Claire	Done

Budget			
Review 1999 budget	Jan	committee	Done
Draft 2000 budget	Jan	committee	Done
Approve 2000 budget	Jan	committee	Done
Invitations			
Draft invitation copy	Jan	Claire	Done
Approve invitation copy	Jan		Done
Produce invitations	Jan	Claire	Done
Get mailing lists from board, Friends, etc.	Jan	Claire	Ongoing
Prepare labels		Claire	Done
Mail invitations and author insert	January	Claire	Done
Comp ticket for photogrpaher			
Comp ticket for Scottoline escort?			
Comp tickets for $1,000+ donors	Feb	Jeanne	
Waiting list for fill-ins	Feb–Mar	Claire	
Program			
Author bios prepared	Jan–Feb	Elizabeth	Done
Winner bios prepared	Jan–Feb	Elizabeth	
Solicit winner tributes for program booklet	Jan–Feb	Omitted	Omit
Write program/agenda text	Jan–Feb	Elizabeth	
Approve program/agenda	Jan–Feb	committee	
Produce program agenda	Jan–Feb	staff	
Produce list of authors, books	Jan–Feb	Claire	
Write script for speakers/ presenters	Jan–Feb	Elizabeth	
Produce signs	Jan–Feb	Claire	
Corporate signs:			
Wells Fargo/book sale		Claire	
Gates/dinner?		Claire	
Covenant/speaker?		Claire	
Miller Hull/authors reception?		Claire	

Foundation banner		Claire	
Table numbers		Claire	
Table names		Claire	
Arrange for photographer		Jeanne/Claire	
Book Sale			
Order books	Jan–Feb	Claire/Julie	
Add McIntyre and children's books	Feb	Claire	
Coordinate book sale setup and volunteers	Feb–Mar	Janet	
Cash for sales	Mar	Claire	
Three imprinters	Mar	Claire	
Credit card slips	Mar	Claire	
Book stands	Mar	Claire	
Plastic bags	Mar	Claire	
Locking cash box with cash drawer	Mar	Claire	
Return unsold books	Mar	Claire	
Two skirted tables for children's books	Mar	Claire	
Thank yous to volunteers	Mar	Claire	
Check-in			
Name tags (plastic sleeves, cards, ribbons)	Mar	Claire	
Name slips for drawings	Mar	Claire	
Author/books list	Mar	Claire	
Author/books placard	Mar	Claire	
Floral arrangement or centerpiece?	Mar	Claire	
Fish bowl for drawing	Mar	Claire	
Three skirted tables			
Assign board members to authors	Mar	Committee	

Post-Event			
Pay bills	Mar	Claire	
Budget	Mar	Claire/Jeanne	
Critique	Mar	Committee	
Report	Mar	Jeanne	
Thank you letters to authors, speaker, emcee, sponsors, etc.	Mar	Claire	

When the event is on the horizon, the lists and timelines get exceedingly specific and crowded with minutiae. One festival organizer prepares a "minute-by-minute" Excel spreadsheet that lists every single thing that happens during the course of the festival, including when it's supposed to be done and who is responsible for doing it. Every task, every team member, every piece of equipment, every location is accounted for in the minute-by-minute.

Another of the challenges of Literary Lions is that a functioning library is turned into a bar and restaurant in the space of two and a half hours. Here's the kind of nitty-gritty detail that Claire keeps track of just before and during the event. This kind of timeline not only keeps Claire on track but lets everyone else involved in accomplishing these tasks know what is expected.

Literary Lions

As a word of explanation, the venue for this event is Bellevue Regional Library, the largest library (80,000 square feet) in King County Library System. The library closes an hour early on Saturday night to allow for Literary Lions transformation. This particular year, the keynoter, Bill Harley, also did a public event the afternoon of the dinner.

Friday, March 11

- Data personnel arrive at 7 A.M. to disconnect cabling.

- Janitorial does preevent cleaning.

- Buildings and Grounds staff moves shelves, tables, equipment, and Choice Reads display units.

- Buildings and Grounds staff installs this year's Literary Lions award winner plate on awards wall above lion statue on staircase landing.

- Buildings and Grounds staff moves Literary Lions supplies in the afternoon from Web services storage area on third floor at Service Center to Board Room at Bellevue Regional Library.

- Caterer delivers rentals between 9 A.M. and noon, rentals stored in Meeting Room 5.

- A/V vendor delivers equipment and rentals around 4:30 P.M., materials stored in Meeting Room 5.

Saturday, March 12

- A/V vendor arrives at 9:30 A.M. to set up for Bill Harley noon concert in Meeting Room 1.

- A/V vendor tears down at approximately 1:30 P.M. and moves to children's area to start setting up for evening program. This includes sound, video, stage, pipe and drape.

- Buildings and Grounds staff hangs sponsor banner on 2nd floor above reference desk. *Note:* sponsor banner is now 5 feet tall by 8 feet wide, which is a different size than previous years.

- Buildings and Grounds staff hangs Literary Lions banner above stage and in front of pipe and drape. Same banner as last year.

- Buildings and Grounds staff moves podium from Meeting Room 1 to stage in children's area.

- Buildings and Grounds staff moves furniture on second floor per Gregg Schiller's floor plan.

- Buildings and Grounds sets up folding tables in gallery and on second floor, per Gregg's floor plan.

  Need twelve tables in Room 5; caterer will set up.

  Need five tables on second floor.

  Need four tables in gallery.

- Caterers arrive around 3 P.M.
- Library closes at 4 P.M.
- Claire on-site from about 11 A.M. to handle product sales at noon program and troubleshoot any developments for evening program.
- Security arrives at 3 P.M. to help clear library and stays until everyone has left, usually by 11:30 P.M. or midnight. Security officer in gallery from 4 P.M. on to admit attendees and discourage library patrons.
- Volunteers arrive between 3:30 and 4:00 P.M. Set up nametag tables and coat check in Meeting Room 1.
- Board members arrive at 6 P.M., guests arrive at 6:30 P.M.
- Dinner and program start at 7:15 P.M.
- ProLine and Cardinal Media staff to handle all A/V matters prior, during and after event.

Sunday, March 13

- Buildings and Grounds move children's furniture back into children's area from storage in truck in the parking lot prior to library opening at noon.
- Janitorial does postevent cleaning.

Monday, March 14

- Rentals (tables, chairs, etc.) stored in Meeting Room 5 are picked up between 9 A.M. and noon.
- A/V vendor returns at 9 A.M. to strike stage, pipe, drape, etc.
- Data personnel arrive at 8 A.M. to reconnect computers, cabling, etc.
- Foundation staff arrives at 10 A.M. to organize supplies going back to SC.
- Buildings and Grounds staff takes down banners. Literary Lions banner to be rolled with lettering facing OUT. Sponsor banner can be disposed of.

- Buildings and Grounds staff moves back shelves, furniture, equipment, etc.
- Buildings and Grounds staff returns supplies in Board Room at Bellevue Regional Library to Web services storage area on third floor at SC.

So if you have your heart set on a really big do, sharpen up a stack of pencils and start making those goals, lists and timelines.

Show Me the Sponsor!

Corporate sponsorship is something that mostly happens just for really big dos. The golden rule of fundraising is that to interest a sponsor in an event, you must clearly demonstrate how your goals match theirs. You must also show the benefits a corporate sponsor would accrue by lending their support to your event.

Lisa A. Wolfe offers guidelines for special event sponsorships in her book *Library Public Relations, Promotions and Communication* published by Neal-Schuman in 2006. She suggests you think carefully about who might be most interested in your event and what companies can actually afford to help you. She reminds librarians that the goodwill and good reputation of a library are strong attractors for businesses and corporations.

Lisa has a sponsorship proposal outline in her book or you can check out a sample request for sponsorship in the Appendix, reprinted by kind permission of Dick Pahle, Development Director for the Public Library of Charlotte and Mecklenberg County.

The Party's Over

Evaluation of a big do is just as essential, if not more so, than evaluation of a less Herculean author event. There's more money, more people, more risk involved. However, it doesn't quite work to hand out evaluation forms at a festival. Who wants to fill out forms at a party? Instead, think about establishing what constitutes success when you begin your planning.

Perhaps it will be attendance, perhaps it will be money raised, perhaps it will be publicity garnered. You can certainly count heads, count dollars and monitor media coverage. The thing to remember about large events is that they may take several years to build an audience, so you have to be prepared to be patient and know what outcome you want.

So now you know some of what's involved in a really big do. They take lots of planning and lots of hard work, but everyone I talked to who has been involved in a big do said they were also big fun.

12

Evaluation and Follow-up

So if you've pulled off a successful author event, go ahead bask in the glow, but you're not done yet. You have a few post-event duties to take care of.

Thanks, Thanks and Thanks

There are a number of people who need to be thanked. It's good manners and it's good insurance if you want to do another event.

First and foremost, thank the author. If you were able to get a mailing address, send it directly to the author. If not, go through the agent or publisher. We would often send along a paperback version of a pictorial book of the area as a souvenir accompanied by a handwritten note. It doesn't have to be lengthy or formal. Here's a sample:

Dear Mark,

Thanks so much for your visit to us here at King County Library System. Our patrons are still buzzing about how much they enjoyed seeing you, and it was a personal treat for me as well.

Please remember we have nearly inexhaustible venues, so should the urge strike to visit the Seattle area again, we are ready, willing and able to host a gracious and talented fellow such as yourself.

With all best wishes to you, Jessica and the new arrival.

Chapple

Second, thank the publicist if you worked through a publishing house. This can be via e-mail. She'll want to know how many people showed up and how it went. She'll also want to know how many books were sold, but I don't like to go there. I leave that to the bookseller. Here's a sample e-mail:

To: Samantha@publishinghouse.com

Subject: Harriet Chessman

Dear Sam,

Harriet's event with our book group members yesterday went swimmingly. Harriet charmed everyone's socks off, just as we knew she would, and had a very attentive, engaged audience of about seventy-five. I noticed that the bookseller was doing a brisk business and everyone seemed eager to talk to Harriet afterward. We were so pleased to have her visit. Thanks so much for making it happen. We'd be glad to have Harriet back anytime.

Chapple

If you held the event in a venue not your own, you should send off a thank you note to the venue manager. Also send a note of appreciation to your ushers, especially if they volunteered their time. And don't forget your bookseller. She's the one who came early and stayed late no matter what the size of the crowd.

I Am Reviewing the Situation

Take a look at your evaluation forms and see what they tell you. What publicity sources paid off particularly well? What should you focus on for future events? If you get some particularly fulsome praise, pull that out to include in your report to the higher-ups along with the head count. There may also be some comments that will be useful in promoting future programs.

I'll confess that I feel quite ambivalent about evaluation forms. I personally hate doing them. In the first place, how likely am I to host this author again? How helpful is it to know that audience thought he mumbled or had an awful tie? I find many evaluation comments speak to issues over which I have no control—the temperature of the room, the hardness of the chairs. We often ask for suggestions for authors to speak. Many times, the authors suggested are well out of our price range, haven't spoken publicly in years or are dead. (Whew, I guess I feel better now.) But putting all my prejudices aside, you need to do it. Too much information always trumps no information at all.

Have a debriefing meeting with your team (include the ushers if you can) and see what worked well and what needs more polish for the next attempt. This is probably the time to review your evaluation form and tweak it so that you're getting the information you really want.

Jane Graham George, who does author events for the Dakota Public Library in Minnesota, has this advice about evaluations:

> Evaluation is an important part of the process. You can determine the success of your programs, the type of audience you are (or are not) attracting, whether your audience consists of frequent library users (or not)—in short, many details that will help you in future planning.
>
> You can make the evaluation form as long or as short as you like, but be aware that your audience may not want to spend a lot of time filling out a lengthy form. Is there anyone who actually *likes* filling out questionnaires? You may want to ask only the important questions, such as:
>
> Did you like the program?
>
> What did you particularly like? What didn't you like?

Are you a regular library user? How often do you visit the library?

What other authors or kinds of programs would you like to see here?

How can we improve programs such as this?

One school district suggests that programmers consider the following questions following and event:

- How can you tell that the program makes a difference?
- What was the most successful aspect of the program? Why?
- What aspect was the most promising? Why?
- What would be the ideal configuration for the program? Why?

You can check in the Appendix for more samples of evaluation forms.

So gather all your data, talk to all your workteam folks and figure out what you did right and what could stand some improvement. Then forge ahead to your next author event.

Here's a sample of an evaluation form Jane has used in Dakota County.

Minnesota Mosaic® Evaluation

1. Do you have a Dakota County Library library card?

    ___ yes   ___ no

2. In the past year, how many times did you visit a library?

    ___ less than four times

    ___ four to six times

    ___ seven to eleven times

    ___ twelve or more times

3. How did you hear about this program?

    ___ Minnesota Mosaic® brochure

    ___ posters at the library

    ___ from another person

    ___ newspaper article

    ___ radio announcement

    ___ other

4. How would you rate this program overall?

    poor   1   2   3   4   5   excellent

5. What did you like best about this program?

6. What would you have changed about this program?

7. Would you attend other Minnesota Mosaic® programs?

8. What other types of library programs do you or would you attend?

9. What other literary programs do you or would you attend at the library?

13

Virtual Visits

Although I'm a great fan of flesh-and-blood events, having an author come in person may not be in the cards for you at this moment in time. You may not be able to come up with any funds for an honorarium and have struck out at making a good match for a "free" author. Perhaps you are far off the flight path of major book tours and haven't been able to coax a publisher to send someone your way. Maybe your community is tech savvy and responds better to a sit-at-home-in-my-sweats event than a get-up-and-go-to-the-library event. Or maybe you just plain don't have a space to do an author event. In such cases you may wish to explore alternative ways of connecting your clientele with authors. This can range from using technology to initiate author programming to taking advantage of what's already out there in the virtual firmament.

Although I'm far from a magician with modern technologies, I'll pass on some of what I've discovered about what can happen without a real, live author in the room. I won't go into much depth in what makes these things happen because that technology will likely be out of date as soon as your coffee cools tomorrow morning. And if you are a technology wizard, you may want to pass this chapter by.

In Latin class (more years ago than I care to remember), I discovered that all Gaul is divided into three parts. Likewise, all virtual communication seems to fall into three categories: text, audio and video.

Text

Probably the text we all think of these days is e-mail and its various communal chat forms. There is live chat, where an author comes online at a specific time to chat in real time to your patrons via some sort of chat client. This may be a particularly comfortable form of communication for authors. After all, composing their thoughts at a keyboard is what they do.

New York Public Library does this with noted writers as part of their summer reading activities for children and teens. They invite teens to join them "wherever they are in the world," and some children's and young adult librarians arrange for kids to gather at the library for these special events. Sandra Payne, Coordinator of Young Adult Services for NYPL, told me about the program:

> Our very first chat was with Sharon Flake, July 2002. Participation system-wide is modest, but those who participate send along good questions for the authors to consider. The chats are moderated here in our offices.
>
> This is right now our sole "virtual" author event. By the way, we would love to do more chats—sometimes we get "original content" through these lively conversations. The authors seem to get a kick out of the events as well. Last summer when the chat ended, I spoke with Meg Cabot, who while in Key West expressed how much she missed New York City–type teens—their snarkiness, their wit. By the way, the fastest typist in the world was Avi! For our chat with Ann M. Martin, we actually had her on the telephone while we typed her responses as she had a computer glitch that day.
>
> All in all—we love the chats!

Salt Lake County Library hosts between three and ten live author chats a month. "It's an inexpensive way to do author events," says program originator Darlene Dineen. "The authors rarely charge us and seem to enjoy chatting with patrons from the comfort of their own computers."

The publishing house Scholastic hosts moderated live author chats throughout the school year aimed at the classroom audience. You can see what they're up to at www.scholastic.com/authorseries.

Barnes & Noble is trying a slightly different approach for its online book club—including the author in an online discussion. To participate, users must sign up online, for free, for classes at "Barnes and Noble University." There are half a dozen or so book clubs offered at any given time. Some of the discussions are comoderated by the author—that's the exciting twist. The discussion opens on a particular date, and members can check in and chat with each other and the author about the book at their own convenience. It's not live chat, and thus you are not bound by a particular time or day.

After the Chat: Transcripts

Many chats are posted on the Web for all to see for some time. New York Public Library has posted its author chats on its Web page for the rest of their readers to enjoy, as has Scholastic. The famous Powell's bookstore in Portland, Oregon, publishes transcripts of their live author interviews. Webmaster Lisa notes that it's perfectly possible to offer e-mail of chat transcripts in an electronic newsletter patrons may request. Transcripts are a step removed, but still a way for patrons to "hear" the author.

The Blogging Life

It took me awhile to get blogs. Correction. I'm still trying to understand the blogging phenomenon. I originally had webloggers pegged as individuals chronicling their private lives for a mass audience. I had a hard time seeing the appeal. I read a number of author blogs and frankly, didn't really care if any of them were having a bad hair day or were on a diet. (I am interested, however, in author Marc Aronson's music collection. Go figure.)

I starting asking the younger members of my staff about the blogs and found out that there was a whole world of bloggers out there who either gave you their take on the world at large or who trolled the Internet for tidbits to pass on to you. Everyone, it seemed, had a blog or two that they checked in with on a regular basis.

Then I discovered that some of these bloggers were making a bundle by selling advertising. If they could document a certain number of viewers they could ask big bucks for ads. (Of course there are about the same ratio of wealthy bloggers as wealthy actors—to a few go the big bucks. The rest starve.) Because many blogs have an easily identified discrete market, blogging, it seems, has become the next big marketing tool. At least until next week …

Like its cousin chat, weblogs are a medium made for writers. Many, many writers have them; as a matter of fact, there is a Web site devoted to authors' blogs: www.authorsblogs.com. The *Internet Writing Journal* has compiled a list of author blogs that they believe to be outstanding. You can check that out at www.internetwritingjournal.com/authorblogs. I was interested to note that at least one library has a list of author blogs on its Web page. It's a way to connect the reader and writer sure enough.

Author blogs hit the news big time, at least in our neck of the woods, when Amazon announced it would host author blogs on "Amazon Connect." Most recent blog posts are featured prominently on the author's profile page or on a book's description page, along with a link to the author's full blog. Marketing pundits are calling this move the online equivalent of an author book signing. Amazon is also offering original work to download for less than a dollar. It's like downloading a tune to your iPod, only you're downloading a short story to your PDA.

I'm also noticing that more and more, authors are blogging cooperatively. "Running with Quills," for instance, is a group blog for Stella Cameron, Jayne Ann Krentz, Elizabeth Lowell and Suzanne Simmons. (There's a mystery blogger in there too, somewhere.) These writers confessed that they didn't have the time or energy to maintain their own blogs, so they banded together in the hope that they could inspire (and nag and harass) each other into maintaining a joint blog.

Audio

I thought exploring the various forms of voice communication would be easy. I soon discovered that my voice communication knowledge was somewhere back roughly in the butter-churn era. More and more voice communication is being tied to data lines and an Internet provider address. (All I know is that when the power goes out, I'm glad to have a fusty old analog phone line.) However your phone works, it is still a viable tool for hosting authors.

It's for You!

Here's a technology we're all so familiar with that we don't even think of it as technology anymore—the phone! Doing an author visit by phone is particularly effective with classes or book groups. Many, many authors offer phone visits on their Web sites. I got an e-mail not long ago from author Susan Vreeland that spoke to her availability to book groups via the phone. One author said she loves to do phone visits because she can wear her pajamas and bunny slippers and no one knows. It seems to me author Adriana Trigiani did a lot of phone visits, especially when she was expecting her first child.

Many publishers make accommodations these days for phone visits. Here's one of HarperCollins promotion pieces.

ATTENTION READING GROUPS!

Invite the Author

Bringing Book Groups and Authors Together

HarperCollins encourages book groups to Invite the Author to their next meeting. Each month, an author and book selection will be announced in the Readers' Roundtable e-newsletter and at www. HarperCollins.com. Authors will participate via telephone with a select number of book groups.

Throughout the spring and summer, acclaimed authors are available to speak via telephone about their books with your book group. A limited number of groups will be selected to participate.

Sign up now for your chance to talk with one of these authors: Mary Kay Andrews, author of *Little Bitty Lies*, and Lionel Shriver, author of *We Need to Talk about Kevin*. And there is still time to enter for conversations with Binnie Kirschenbaum, author of *Disturbance in One Place*; William Lashner, author of *Past Due*; and Kathleen Tessaro, author of *Elegance*.

Go to http://www.harpercollins.com/hc/readers/invite.asp for more information and your chance to Invite the Author!

As I mentioned earlier, the difference between voice lines and data lines are beginning to blur. Once upon a time, "Touch Tone Tales" were six-minute stories that children could dial up by phone to hear. Now, at our library, they have been transferred to the Web so that children can listen at the computer—or download them to the MP3 players. It seems to me this is a technique could be used with authors as well.

Podcasting

I heard on the news the other day that the number of podcasts is doubling every month. If you've got speakers, a microphone and a broadband connection, you're in business.

A growing number of libraries are starting to hop on the podcast bandwagon. Fairfax County Public Library in Virginia offers BookCast, a series of podcast interviews with local authors. The Public Library of Charlotte and Mecklenburg County in North Carolina also offers news, programs and commentary created for and by teens at www.libraryloft.org.

Simon & Schuster has also picked up on the podcasting phenomena and now offers weekly podcasts of their authors. You can check it out on their Web site, www.simonsays.com.

Video

Most libraries use video as an extension of their in-person author event. In conjunction with their local government access public access channel, they broadcast their program to an overflow crowd in another room or to viewers of that channel. It's much the same as televised City Council meetings—though surely much more compelling. As I mentioned earlier, some libraries then add the tapes or CDs of the program to the collection so that patrons may check them out.

There are some Web sites that have snippets of authors on video. Penguin publishers say they have video with interviews with their authors on their Web site, http://us.penguingroup.com/static/html/video.html. Sometimes it really is a video interview, and sometimes it's an audio interview with photos of the author. Bookwrapcentral.com, on the other hand, has brief but engaging videos of author interviews that you can host on your own Web site.

You can also purchase services such as www.teachingbooks.net that offer original author programs in the form of a five-minute video of the author. Geared for the school market, teachingbooks.com offers a host of supplemental materials, including excerpts of books read by the author or a professional actor.

Most original video of author events that I've seen is done by big guns, like BookTV. Because video files are so big, they are pricey to send and receive. One friend told me with some force that video is unrealistic for everyone but Bill Gates. And by the way, he said, line TV as we know it will be dead in five years—it will all be Web based. Whoever thought the day would come when we'd think of television as quaint?

So there you have it, some thoughts about how to connect with an author when a flesh-and-blood event isn't in the cards. As the market and technology changes, prices and delivery systems will change. So if this avenue captures your fancy, keep your eyes and ears open because I'm sure between the time I write this and you read, it there'll be dozens more ways.

14

Tips for Authors

Okay, authors, I don't know how you landed here, but stay tuned for a little friendly advice. Publishing is a tough biz, granted, and not many publishers make any attempt to publicize or promote much of their list anymore, so it's up to you. And here you are at home wondering how you can get some exposure or on the road, touting your book. It may or may not be a comfortable position for you. You may devoutly wish you were back in your study writing away. But you're here. Here are some tips not only to help you get out there but to make you beloved of the booksellers, librarians and event planners with whom you come in contact. Listen up.

Get on the Shelf

All those lovelorn ballads to the contrary, this is one instance in which you really do want to be on the shelf, at least you want your *book* on the shelf. So before you do anything about trying to arrange a reading at your local library, make sure the library owns your book. This will give you some credibility as an author of merit.

Looking on the library shelf isn't necessarily going to give you the answer for this one. You'll need to look in the library's catalog. The catalog will likely be computerized and will just as likely be available to you via the Internet on the library's Web site. Log on and see if you are listed in the author index. (If you are, you've just discovered a consistent source of cheap thrills. It's pretty exciting to find yourself in the library catalog.) Pay attention when you're looking in the catalog. How many libraries seem to be represented in those holdings? Is it just your hometown library, or are other libraries' locations listed there as well? That will be your first clue to the library's administrative structure. That's the next thing you need to research.

Poke around on the library's Web site a little more and see what you can find out. It may be a stand-alone city library, it may be a branch of a large metropolitan library, it may be a county library system with many branches, or it may be an independent library that's part of a county or state consortium. See if you can find the part of the Web site that explains the library administration. If the Apple Valley Library is a part of the Fruitvale Library System, then you'll just want to know that there is a copy or two of your book in the system somewhere that Apple Valley residents have access to.

If you didn't find your book in the library's catalog, you have some work to do. First you need to find out who does the book selection for your library or library system so that you can make sure your book is considered for purchase. In a big library system, books are often selected by librarians at central administrative offices, not in the community libraries, so don't assume whoever happens to be at a public service desk is in a position to buy your book. Ask who and where the selector is and call him or her. When you call, you will be better received if you don't do a heavy sales job about your book. Rather, request information about having your book purchased. (Librarians are all about giving out information; you'll be speaking their language.)

Most libraries have selection guidelines that they adhere to and have standard policies about what prerequisites they require before they buy a book. It might be a certain number of reviews, it might be that a selector personally looks at a book, it might be local interest. Here's the information King County Library System gives to authors who want to their books to be considered for purchase:

Marketing Your Book to King County Library System

For Small Presses and Local Authors

King County Library System actively seeks books that are written and/or published locally. We are especially interested in those about the Pacific Northwest. As a public library, we select books whose content is written for the general reader rather than for the specialist or practitioner. We do not collect textbooks. Books with pages designed to be filled in by the reader, or torn out, are not appropriate.

Because books in a public library get heavy and sometimes careless use from the public, we look for ones that are sturdily bound, preferably sewn or glued. Spiral and comb bindings do not stand up well in our setting.

The best way to bring your book our attention is through reviews. A positive review in one or more of the library review journals, such as *Library Journal, School Library Journal* (for children's books,) *Kirkus, Booklist* or *Publisher's Weekly* or in *The Seattle Times* Sunday Northwest books review section will give your book an excellent chance of being bought by KCLS (and other public libraries as well.) See below for more information on the publications.

The next best method is a flyer mailed to the KCLS Service Center. Librarians generally have only a few seconds to look at a flyer, so your best bet is to emphasize the essentials. We look for:

- WHAT the book is about. This should be brief and pithy.

- WHY the book is needed at KCLS. Here you should include quotations from reviews or reader testimonials if you have them. If the book has been reviewed, you could also attach a copy of the review or citation to it.

- WHO the intended audience is for this book. Is it intended for adults, young adults or children? Parents, businesspersons, hobbyists, etc.?

- WHO the author is. This should include qualifications, such as education, experience in the field, and experience as a writer. Be sure to mention that you are a local author or publisher, since this is a factor in our decision whether to buy.

- WHEN, WHERE, etc. the book was published. We need all the bibliographic data, including date of publication, price, ISBN number (very important), edition statement, type of binding. If the book is self-published, please give some indication of its physical appearance, including how it is bound.

- HOW we can get it. Libraries prefer to buy from wholesale vendors, such as Ingram, Brodart, Baker and Taylor, or, locally, Partners West or Koen Pacific. There are also national vendors that specialize in small press books, including Quality Books and Unique Books. If the book is only available directly from you, be sure to provide a phone number, address, and e-mail address if you have one. Be prepared to accept purchase orders and to wait several weeks for payment.

A sample copy of the book sent with the preceding information is helpful to us, but not necessary.

If you have a Web page that describes your book and includes all of the above information, you can e-mail the URL for it to: selector@kcls.org. Or you can send an e-mail with the information to that same address.

Drop-in visits are not encouraged. Our schedules are crowded, and you may end up wasting your time if no one is available when you arrive.

You may also want to consider being an exhibitor at library conferences. This is one way to reach many librarians in a short space of time. National conference such as the American Library Association can be overwhelming, but smaller ones such as Pacific Northwest Library Association and Washington Library Association attract many librarians from this area. See additional information below.

Contacts

Send flyers to:

Selection Department
King County Library System
960 Newport Way NW
Issaquah, WA 98027
For Information on how to submit a book for a review:

Booklist
50 East Huron Street
Chicago, IL 60611
http://www.ala.org/booklist/submit.html

Kirkus
200 Park Avenue South
New York, NY 10003
https://www.kirkusreviews.com

Library Journal
245 West 17th St.
New York, NY 10011
http://www.bookwire.com/ljdigital/about.htm

Publisher's Weekly
245 W. 17th St.
New York, NY 10011
http://www.bookwire.com/pw/general.html#SUBMITTING

Library Organizations

The American Library Association events Web Page (http://www.ala.org/events) lists upcoming conferences. Information on exhibiting at each conference is available through the links for the individual events.

Pacific Northwest Library Association (PNLA) has a Web page (www.pnla.org) that lists links to all of its member associations and lists upcoming conferences.

For the Washington Library Association, see http://www.wla.org/conf.html.

Small Press Vendors

Quality Books
    1003 W. Pines Road
    Oregon, IL 61061-9680
    (800) 323-4241

Unique Books
    5010 Kemper Ave.
    St. Louis, MO 62139
    (800) 533-5446

LOCAL VENDORS

Koen Pacific
    18249 Olympic Avenue S.
    Tukwila, WA 98188-4722
    (206) 575-7544

Partners West
    1901 Raymond Avenue SW, Suite C
    Renton, WA 98055
    (800) 563-2385

Once you understand the process, you can take the steps necessary to get your book included in the collection. Be polite and professional. **Important note:** even if you just want to give your book to the library, the same steps will often apply. I cannot tell you how many times I get an unsolicited copy of a book with a note that says, "Hi, I'm Hans Gunther and I just wrote this terrific book on ballroom dancing that I want you to have."

On the surface, it seems like a great, even generous, thing to do. In real library life, it's a pain in the neck. In the first place, I don't do book selection for our library so I'm the wrong person to send your book to. Second, not very many libraries are going to accept a gift without some sort of evaluation. I need a sound basis for adding your book to the collection so that when, down the line, someone waves your book in my face and hollers that it's the WORST book on ballroom dancing she's ever seen and her partner broke his foot trying to follow the directions to the rhumba, I have a rationale for why it was added to the collection. It's at that point that I want a couple of terrific reviews in my pocket or at least a selector's careful evaluation of the book.

In the third place, especially for a big library system, adding just one copy of a book is like stopping an assembly line to screw on a single part. It makes the costs for processing and cataloging very high. And then if that one book goes missing, you have to spend staff time (i.e., money) deleting that catalog record. Libraries often deal with vendors who partially process or catalog the book for them. If your book doesn't go through that process, you are creating additional work for the library. That's another obstacle for you to overcome. To use a car analogy, a dealer receives shiny new cars ready to be sold and driven off the lot. That dealer would not be very keen to receive a car from a different source that he would have to repaint or invest a lot of work into before he could sell it.

Having now given you every cautionary under the sun, let me just say that libraries love their local authors and most take great pains to make sure they are represented in the collection. So if you find out first what the rules are and play by them, you are likely to be welcomed with open arms.

Getting In

Now that your book is in the library, it's time to make a pitch for your event. Before you take that step, do a little more research. You can do part of this online, but you really need to go take a look at the library at some point in the process. You've already determined the library's administrative structure, so you know whether they are a stand-alone library or part of a system. Now you need to pick up a little library jargon. A library "program" is an event put on by the library for the public. It may be anything from a preschool storytime to a book club for teens to an opera preview to an author reading. When a librarian talks about programming, that's what she means.

So now go down to the library and see if you can answer these questions.

- Is there a library meeting room?

- If there isn't a meeting room or community room, then it's difficult for a library to host any sort of event. Some libraries may offer special programs, especially for children, at the community center or the firehall next door. As a rule, if there's no room for programs, programs don't happen on a regular basis.

- Does the library already do programming on a regular basis?

- Look for posters and flyers that advertise library events. This is also a good thing to look for on the Web page.

- Does there seem to be an emphasis on any particular service or clientele? For instance, right now early literacy is a very hot topic for our library. If you were looking around, you might be able to tell that from the programs we offer, from the banners on the wall and from the tags on our badges that say "Ask Me about Early Literacy." If any author approached me with a program that tied his book into getting prereaders ready to read, I'd be on that program like a proverbial duck on the June bug.

The next question you'll need to resolve will take more than just looking around. You'll probably have to ask, "Who does the programming?" In our library system, there are several programming tracks. The children's staff plans and executes storytimes and other programs for children. They may also hire performers and others to offer programs to children. We also have a librarian who arranges for programs for adults … in addition to her other duties. She's the one who will make local arrangements for the aforementioned opera previews or talks on travel in Tuscany. We are a big system, so we also have a person who does programming centrally. That means she'll arrange for every library to have a certain number of programs during the summer in conjunction with our summer reading program. She'll also put together the programs for Poetry Month or Teen Read Week or whatever else the library system decides to do. If you were to go through her to do a reading, you'll need to be prepared to do your thing at a number of libraries.

Pitching Your Act

Once you know who does the programming for the library, you can approach her about hosting an author event. Before you start your pitch, however, make sure you have everything a programmer will want. Put together a press kit that includes:

- Book cover
- Author photo
- Short description of the book
- Long description of the book
- Credits, previous books
- Author bio
- Reviews
- Business card
- Description of your program
- Copy of your book (optional)

Once you have your press kit together, it's time to approach a program planner.

Here's an e-mail I received from an author that captured my attention because it showed she'd done some homework. Her attachment included contact information, reviews of the book and the bookjacket cover.

To: Chapple Langemack   **From:** Joyce Yarrow

Subject: Reading at the King County Library System

I'm very pleased to see that the King County Library has purchased six copies of my mystery novel, *Ask the Dead*, and that they are all checked out :).

I'm making myself available to talk at local libraries and would appreciate your forwarding this e-mail and its attachment to your programming coordinator. The talks are informal and topics covered include: putting the "who" in who done it; strengthening characters through sense of place; creating characters from personal experience.

Thanks for your time and consideration.

Cordially,

Joyce Yarrow

As Public Programming Coordinator for King County Library System, Deborah Schneider develops those "central" programs I mentioned earlier. She says when an author calls and says they want to do "a reading," she can barely hear them over her yawns. She likes it when authors put some effort into developing a fun and interesting program.

Here's an example. Charlie Williams, a performer known as "The Noise Guy," just self-published *Flush: An Ode to Toilets,* a rhyming restroom tour. He asked to have his launch party (appropriately named "Flush Fest") in a library meeting room. I didn't go, but I was certainly invited (along with everyone else in the library system), and I've heard about it nonstop ever since. Charlie and his wife outdid themselves decorating the room. There was toilet paper everywhere. Big balloon arches were anchored by real, live toilets planted with floral arrangements. Guests signed in on the stall wall and could have their picture taken with their head in a cartoon toilet. The pièce de résistance was an ice sculpture toilet with a suspicious looking chemical-blue punch in the bowl. Charlie not only performed, he involved the crowd with games like "TP the librarian" and prizes such as a pallet of toilet paper. This unknown (self-published!) author drew a crowd of more than a hundred, plus the newspaper, plus a camera crew from one of the local television magazine shows. He and his wife did all the work (and cleaned up), and the library got to bask in reflected glory. That's a great author event.

While toilets may not be your thing, be creative with your own topic and see what you can come up with to add some excitement to your event.

Getting Your Act Together

Once you've scored an author event, be it a library or anywhere else, it's time to turn your attention to your performance. Debbie's advice is not to be afraid to be different. Think about setting the stage with music or interesting clothing as well as what you're going to say.

Speak the Speech, I Pray You

If you're not comfortable speaking in front of people, get help. Find a media coach like Kim Dwyer or read a book like *Naked at the Podium* by Melanie Workhoven. (Find out more about these two in the Additional Resources section at the end of the book.) When it's painful for you, it's painful for us, the audience. Do not read your speech. Not everybody has to be Mr. Spectacular, but please, make an honest effort or stay home and blog.

Plan and Prepare

Plan your presentation. Reading from your work is fine up to a point. What we really want to know is how the book happened. What inspired you to go to all the work of writing the book? How did you do your research? Is there something unusual about your protagonist? What did you learn about yourself as you wrote this book? Did you bring personal experience into the story?

Read from your work if it's illustrative of a point you want to make, but don't go overboard. No offense, but we can read the book ourselves. If you give us everything, what motivation do we have to buy the book? One bookseller told me that one of the most interesting author events she witnessed was when an author read (briefly) from the work that inspired him to write his own book.

Now I have to tell you that a writer friend of mine took issue with my advice to read sparingly. "That's why I go to author events," she cried plaintively. "I *want* to hear the writer read from his work." So now you've heard from all sides.

If you choose to read from your work, prepare it ahead of time. Think about reading several shorter selections instead of one long one. Go for something memorable, something that tugs at the emotions rather than an example of finely crafted prose. Read through it; mark up the page with where you need to take a breath, where you need to put emphasis. Use that same book or document each time, so your preparation is in front of you. Now develop a short introduction to use before you read your sections.

It's a tough thing to get excited all over again about a book that you were done with two years ago, but you need to make the effort to get back into that place no matter what your current project is.

It's true that weird things happen and sometimes you have to deviate from your plan, but it's so much better to be prepared to begin with.

Make Your Needs Known

If there are things that make you uncomfortable, say so upfront. Tell the event planner what you need. I want to do everything I can to make your visit a good one, it's so much easier if you let me know *in advance* what you need.

Check in with the event planner a day or two before and check in. Make sure equipment for a PowerPoint presentation is available (God, forbid) if that's what you need. Call from the airport if that's what it takes. A day before I can do something about it. Five minutes before the event, it's not likely I can. You'll also relieve the mind of the planner that you are really coming.

Help Promote the Event

Be willing to do media. It's your book we're trying to sell here. If you have a Web page or a blog, make sure the event is mentioned. Let your friends know you're coming. Maybe your cousin in Atlanta has a friend in Seattle who would just love to come and hear you. Let everyone know where you'll be.

Go with the Flow

Learn how to deal with different-sized groups. We event planners try as hard as we can to promote your event. Sometimes, despite our best efforts, only six people show up. If that happens, be gracious. Do something appropriate to the size of the crowd. Have everyone pull up a chair and talk together. We recently hosted first novelist Jim Lynch. The attendance was very disappointing, but Jim was not. Everyone who came was very enthusiastic about his book and thrilled to be able to meet him. The informal discussion was great, and everyone bought at least one copy of *The Highest Tide*. How can that not be a successful event?

If You Can't Say Something Nice ...

I know that book tours are a grind. I know that you have to deal with more than your share of dunderheads. I know that aggravations and inconveniences are common. I know that you are really, really tired and wish you were home. But still, when you are in my town, in my library, be nice. We are predisposed to love you or we wouldn't have invited you. Don't let us down.

If you have complaints, let the appropriate person know, don't broadcast them from the podium. Please don't, as one author did, begin your presentation by grumpily saying, "I don't know where I am or why I'm here." That may well be the case, but we're here. We like it here. We want you to be glad to be here and pleased to see us. Please don't, as one author did, lambast the event planner and the bookseller for not having one obscure title of yours for sale. We did the best we could. Wasn't it your current book that you wanted to promote? Please don't denigrate other authors. It's embarrassing and uncomfortable and doesn't help your cause. Even if you're tired beyond breath of being compared to Author X, don't say he's a raving lunatic.

Grace under pressure is something we'll love you for forever. Booksellers will handsell your books like crazy and librarians will recommend you until the cows come home. Someone once brought up *Angela's Ashes* for Malachy McCourt to sign. I gasped; it seemed very rude. Malachy took it in stride, signed his brother's book politely and moved on. A bookseller told me that Daniel Handler (Lemony Snicket to you and me) was speaking to a huge crowd of kids when a little boy in the front row, excited beyond bearing to be there, threw up. Daniel, the consummate professional, handled it in the best Lemony Snicket manner and moved on. (And don't you wish you could have seen it?) My undying gratitude goes to those authors who signed and signed and signed no matter how long the queue, who greeted their readers with respect and warmth. Those authors who understand how special it is for us to meet them. It may be tedious repetition to you, but it's a once in a lifetime event for us.

Take an Active Role

Work with your host for an event. Find out who your audience is and what the rules of engagement are. Know how long you're supposed to talk. Learn to cut off questions yourself. We'll help you in any way we can, but it's tiresome to always be the bad guy, especially when you say, "Well, I guess they're going to make me stop now."

Mind Your Manners

Remember the "little people" when you're visiting. When Rick Bragg did an event at the Burien Library, he walked through the workroom and spoke to the pages and library assistants. They talk about that to this day. I hear Anthony Bourdain goes into the kitchen and speaks Spanish with the crew then goes out in the alley and smokes with the dishwasher. He may be a crazy man, but everyone loves him.

Thank your host. Thank the booksellers. Ask for a business card and write a follow-up thank you note. It'll make a big impression, and we'll be your slaves forever. A bookseller friend who has been doing author events for years says she's only ever received about five thank you notes. Some of the biggest names in the business manage to do it even with crushing book tour schedules.

Having thrown all these cautionaries out there, let me just say the 99.9 percent of you are already doing great. You come gladly—when you're supposed to—you give it your all and thank us for our efforts. For that I thank you on behalf of author event planners everywhere. It is a special thing for us, and we love it. We love you. After all, authors are magical beings.

Appendix

Sample Event Fact Sheet

Literary Lions Gala

Who: The King County Library System Foundation

Where: Bellevue Regional Library

1111 110th NE, Bellevue, Washingotn
425.450.1765
http://www.kcls.org/brl/bellgen.cfm (for directions to library)

When: 6:30 p.m. on **Saturday, March 11, 2006**

Why: To raise funds for Early Literacy outreach programs that help children arrive at their first day of school ready to read and ready to learn.
To honor individuals and/or organizations and companies that promote literacy and lifelong learning in our communities.
To recognize contributions from more than two dozen Northwest authors.

What: • From 6:30 to 7 P.M., enjoy hors d'oeuvres and wine while you chat with the authors and browse through a selection of their titles at the benefit book sale.

• From 7 to 9 P.M. join friends and colleagues for dinner. Each table will feature a Northwest author.

• The program, including presentation of the 2006 Literary Lions Award to the **Talaris Research Institute,** is followed by an entertaining and thought-provoking address by author and corporate consultant **Kevin Carroll.**

167

After the program, enjoy chocolates, coffee, and champagne while you stock up on more books and chat with the authors.

Founded by Jolene and Bruce McCaw, the **Talaris Research Institute** works to improve the social, emotional, and cognitive development of children from the prenatal period through age five, by providing parents with research-based information they can use in their every day parenting decisions. Talaris, in partnership with KCTS/Seattle, developed the *Parenting Counts* program consisting of television spots, workshop curricula, and collateral materials for use by participating PBS stations across the country. The latest *Parenting Counts* material focuses on how literacy develops and the role that parents play in helping their child learn.

After overcoming childhood obstacles, **Kevin Carroll** built a career as an Army linguist and college and professional sports athletic trainer. Basketball coach Phil Knight tapped Carroll to bring his life and work experiences to Nike, where Carroll was the company "Katalyst" (someone who brings creative ideas into reality) and Master Storyteller. Since then, Carroll has worked with organizations such as Starbucks, The Discovery Channel, ESPN, HSBC Bank, Mattel, Capital One, and The National Hockey League to promote the power of play and creativity in achieving maximum human potential. He is the founder of The Katalyst Consultancy and the author of *Rules of the Red Rubber Ball: Find and Sustain Your Life's Work*.

Previous Award Winners

2005 Gloria and Ted Rand

2004 Page Ahead

2003 The Starbucks Foundation

2002 Verizon Reads program

2001 Ron Sher, Third Place Books, and Eastside Literacy Council

2000 Microsoft Corporation and the Bill & Melinda Gates Foundation; Seattle Goodwill Adult Basic Education; and Bill Ptacek, KCLS Director

1999 Ron Sims, King County Executive, and Tacoma Community House

1998 Kitty Harmon, Northwest BookFest, and Washington Mutual Bank

1997 John Stanford, Seattle Public Schools Superintendent, and Davis Wright Tremaine

1996 Julia Shaw, Eastside Literacy Council Board & National Laubach Board, and United Parcel Service Foundation

1995 Mari and Malcolm Stamper, Storytellers Ink

1994 Washington State Lt. Gov. Joel Pritchard, Washington Reads

Confirmed Guest Authors

Donna Anders—*Another Life*

Greg Atkinson—*Entertaining in the Northwest Style*

Peter Bacho—*Entrys*

Marianne Binetti—*Best Garden Plants for Washington and Oregon*

Matt Briggs—*Shoot the Buffalo*

Carmela & Steve D'Amico—*Ella Takes the Cake*

Alexandra Day—*Carl's Sleepy Afternoon*

Janet Lee Carey—*The Double Life of Zoe Flynn*

Charles R. Cross—*Room Full of Mirrors*

Clyde W. Ford—*The Long Mile*

Michael Gruber—*The Witch's Boy*

Michael Hoeye—*No Time Like Show Time*

Stephanie Kallos—*Broken for You*

Laura McGee Kvasnosky—*Zelda and Ivy and the Boy Next Door*

Martin Limón—*The Door to Bitterness*

Jim Lynch—*The Highest Tide*

Margaret Read MacDonald—*The Squeaky Door*

Cynthia Nims—*Salmon*

Jane Porter—*The Frog Prince*

Gloria Rand—*A Pen Pal for Max*

Carole Lexa Schaefer—*The Bora-Bora Dress*

Jennie Shortridge—*Eating Heaven*

Brad Thiessen—*Orso: The Troll Who Couldn't Scare*

Andrea Rains Waggener—*Alternate Beauty*

Marty Wingate—*The Big Book of Northwest Perennials*

For more information contact: Claire Wilkinson, KCLS Foundation
425.369.3448; cwilkins@kcls.org

Sample Sponsor Proposal

*"A library outranks any one thing a community
can do to benefit its people."*

—Andrew Carnegie

The Hearst Corporation and the Public Library of Charlotte & Mecklenburg
County

2005 Sponsorship Proposal

July 6, 2005

The Hearst Corporation and the Public Library have enjoyed a close association for more than a decade.

For more than a decade, Hearst Corporation has been a valued sponsor of the award-winning *Novello Festival of Reading*.

With the opening of *ImaginOn: The Joe & Joan Martin Center*, 2005 will be an extraordinary year for the Library. Dovetailing with this facility grand opening will be the fifteenth annual *Novello Festival of Reading*.

Most *Novello* events will take place in *ImaginOn*'s state of the art theatres, adding considerably to the popularity of and excitement for this year's *Festival*.

What follows are the details of a proposal that highlight the benefits of association with this year's *Novello Festival of Reading*.

As sponsor of *Novello*, the Hearst Corporation will enjoy the following benefits:

- Logo placement on all print promotional material including newspaper advertisements, brochures, website and event signage.
- Tickets to every ticketed event (not all *Novello* events require tickets)
- Opportunity to attend private, sponsor only reception with Andrea Mitchell (see grant request below).
- Logo recognition on signage at WordPlay Saturday. This year's WordPlay will take place on the *ImaginOn* grounds and will be scheduled to coincide with the ribbon cutting ceremony.

We anticipate this year's WordPlay Saturday attendance to be 6,000, or more. Many attendees will be dignitaries, elected officials and community leaders.

2005 Novello Schedule of Events

WordPlay Saturday—Saturday, October 8, 10 A.M.–4 P.M.
A family festival for children of all ages. Will take place on the grounds of ImaginOn and coincide with the eagerly anticipated grand opening.

Literary Adventure—Thursday and Friday, October 20 and 21
Children's book writers and illustrators visit area schools.

Writing Workshop with Robin Edgar—Monday, October 17
This workshop will focus on use of memories in ones writing.

Poetry Workshop with Jaki-Shelton Green—Tuesday, October 18
Poetry workshops are always popular Novello offerings.

Fiction Workshop with Judy Goldman—Thursday, October 20
Judy Goldman is popular local novelist and frequent commentator on WFAE.

Novello Evening with Peter Reinhart—Thursday, October 20
Writings and reflections from an acclaimed baker and teacher (Johnson & Wales). Author of numerous books on food including *The Bread Makers Apprentice: Mastering The Art of Extraordinary Bread and American Pie: My Search for the Perfect Pizza.*

Novello Evening with Chris Bohjalian—Friday, October 21
Best-selling author of nine novels, including *Midwives*, an Oprah Book Club Selection. His newest novel, *Before You Know Kindness*, was called "one of the funniest, best-written, most compassionate, most engaging, and flat-out most enjoyable novels I've ever read" by Howard Frank Mosher.

Novello Evening with Andrea Mitchell—Saturday, October 22
Chief Foreign Affairs Correspondent for NBC News. She reports on evolving foreign policy issues in the United States and abroad for all NBC News broadcasts, including Nightly News with Brian Williams, Today and for MSNBC.

Novello Evening with Robert Whitlow—Monday, October 24
It has taken Robert Whitlow less than a decade to become one of America's leading fiction writers. Since 2000, he has released four acclaimed legal suspense novels: *The List, The Sacrifice* and *The Trial. The Trial* won a Christy Award in the Contemporary Christian Fiction category.

Novello Press Night—Tuesday, October 25
> Formerly Carolina Writers Night. This year's event features the one-of-a-kind South Carolina farmer and writer, Dori Sanders.
> Novello Evening with Michael Schwalbe—Wednesday, October 26
> An Associate Professor of Sociology at North Carolina State University. Author of numerous books, his latest is *Remembering Root & Shine*, a novel about two working-class African Americans who lived and died in the American South.

Novello Evening with Elizabeth Berg—Thursday, October 27
> Author of ten national best-selling novels, including the New York Times best sellers *True to Form*, *Never Change*, and *Open House*, an Oprah Book Club Selection. Two others, Durable Goods and Joy School, were selected as American Library Association Best Books of the Year.

Novello Evening with Sandra Guzman—Saturday, October 29
> Editor-in-Chief of *Latina* magazine, Ms. Guzman is an award-winning journalist with more than ten years experience in newspapers and television. As the dynamic leader of the firstbilingual lifestyle magazine for Hispanic women, Ms. Guzman gives a voice to all Latinas nationwide.

Grant Request

Traditionally, Hearst's sponsorship of *Novello* has been at the "supporting sponsorship level" of $2,000. On occasions when there has been a private reception with a special *Novello* guest, the grant amount increased to $3,000.

This year's *Novello* will feature a private, sponsor only reception with Andrea Mitchell. A three thousand dollar sponsorship grant would provide for two tickets to attend this private reception, to be held in *ImaginOn*.

Sample Evaluation Form

Tell Us More ...

Are you an adult _____ or child _____? (Please list your age) _____

What program did you participate in?_____

Where did you attend this program? _____

If this is a program for children or teens, did you think this program was:

Too Young _____ Too Old_____ or Just Right _____

On a scale of 1 to 10, with 10 being high, how would your rate the quality of this program?   10 9 8 7 6 5 4 3 2 1

How would you rate your enjoyment of this program?

       10 9 8 7 6 5 4 3 2 1

What did you enjoy about the program?

What made this program less enjoyable for you?

Would you participate again if this program was repeated? Yes ___ No___

How did you hear about this program?

     ___ Library staff

     ___ Flyer picked up at the library

     ___ Mailed flyer or e-mail message

     ___ KCLS Web site

     ___ TV/radio/newspaper ad _____

     ___ Other. Please Specify _____

Please send me information about future author programs at KCLS

Name: _____

By mail_____

_____

Or via e-mail _____

Thank you for your input!

Additional Resources

More about Programming

Buzzeo, Toni, and Jane Kurtz. *Terrific Connections with Authors, Illustrators, and Storytellers: Real Space and Virtual Links.* Englewood, CO: Libraries Unlimited, 1999.

> Covers the nuts and bolts of author school visits—including how students might use alternative methods to make contact with an author.

Lear, Brett W. *Adult Programs in the Library.* Chicago: American Library Association, 2002.

> A good resource for developing guidelines, finding funding and generating publicity for adult programs. Also includes suggestions for evaluation.

Phelps, Thomas C., and Peggy O'Donnell. *Humanities Programming: A How-to-Do-It Manual for Librarians.* New York: Neal-Schuman, 1997.

> Considers every aspect of the process, from idea development and interagency collaboration to fundraising and evaluation. Also included are examples of successful programs from across the country and winning National Endowment of Humanities proposals.

Robertson, Deborah A. *Cultural Programming for Libraries: Linking Libraries, Communities and Culture.* Chicago: American Library Association, 2005

> Deb Robertson is the head of ALA's Public Programming Office. She covers planning and evaluating your program, collaborating with other agencies, funding and marketing your program. She has scores of examples of success series, formats and themes.

More Resources for Finding Authors

> • **Authors @ Your Library:** http://www.authorsatyourlibrary.org/
>
> > Sponsored by Association of American Publishers in concert with the American Library Association, Friends of Libraries

175

USA (FOLUSA) and the *Library Journal,* this Web site is a free online matchmaking service that links publishers and librarians to simplify the process of scheduling library events. Authors @ Your Library has been developed for librarians who want to easily schedule successful author events, and for publishers who are seeking enthusiastic audiences for their authors.

- **Authors on the Web:** https://www.authorsontheweb.com

    This Web site is a product of the folks who do bookreporter.com. It lists forthcoming and recent releases, author roundtables and links to many author Web sites.

- **Society of Children's Book Authors and Illustrators:** http://www.scbwi.org/

    The SCBWI acts as a network for the exchange of knowledge between writers, illustrators, editors, publishers, agents, librarians, educators, booksellers and others involved with literature for young people. There are currently more than 19,000 members worldwide, in more than 70 regions, making it the largest children's writing organization in the world.

- **Poets and Writers Inc. Staff.** 2003. *A Directory of American Poets and Fiction Writers.* New York: Poets and Writers, Inc.

    Poets & Writers, Inc. is the primary source of information, support, and guidance for creative writers. The most current directory is online at http://www.pw.org/directry/

- **Fiction_L** (Listserve): http://www.webrary.org/rs/flsubunsub.html

    An electronic mailing list devoted to reader's advisory topics such as book discussions, booktalks, collection development issues, booklists and bibliographies and a wide variety of other topics of interest to librarians, book discussion leaders and others with an interest in reader's advisory. The discussion is not limited to fiction but rather covers all aspects of reader's advisory for children, young adults and adults, including nonfiction materials.

Look at the following publications for information on authors and publishers:

Publishers Weekly
245 West 17th Street
New York, NY 10011
(212) 463.6782

Booklist Magazine
50 East Huron Street
Chicago, IL 60611
(800) 545.2433

Library Journal
245 West 17th Street
New York, NY 10011
(212) 463.6818

The New York Times Book Review
229 West 43rd Street
New York, NY 10036
(212) 556.7267

More about Publicity and Marketing

Goldstein, Norm, editor. *Associated Press Stylebook and Briefing on Media Law*. Published annually. Cambridge, MA: Perseus, 2006.
 This is the bible of newspaper writing. It will tell you how to punctuate, abbreviate and darn near anything else.

Walters, Suzanne. *Marketing: A How-to-Do-It Manual for Librarians*. New York: Neal-Schuman, 1992.
 Covers the principles of marketing and market research—otherwise known as finding your audience and putting a message across to them.

Wolfe, Lisa A. *Library Public Relations, Promotions, and Communications: A How-to-Do-It Manual*. 2nd ed. New York: Neal-Schuman, 2005.
 Everything you ever wanted to know about publicizing programs, plus helpful information on special events.

More about Fundraising and Grant Writing

Murtz, John, and Katherine Murray. *Fundraising for Dummies*. 2nd ed. Hoboken, NJ: Wiley, 2006
 Includes organizing your fundraising team, writing winning grant proposals and special events in person and on the Web.

Swan, James. *Fundraising for Libraries: 25 Proven Ways to Get More Money for Your Library*. New York: Neal-Schuman, 2002.

> Swan clearly establishes the fundamentals of fundraising and grant writing and provides guidelines for any number of fundraising events including special author events.

Wendroff, Alan L. *Special Events: Proven Strategies for Nonprofit Fundraising*. 2nd ed. Hoboken, NJ: Wiley, 2004.

> Who is the audience for my event? How much can I charge? These questions and many others are covered in meticulous detail by this book and CD-ROM.

More about Presentation Skills

Kahle, Peter V. T., and Melanie Workhove. *Naked at the Podium: The Writer's Guide to Successful Readings*. Seattle, WA: 74th Street Productions, 2001.

> This how-to for writers on tour promoting their work has lots of presentation tips.

Kim from L.A. Literary & Media Services: www.KimfromLA.com

> For authors who want help with a lecture or presentation. Kim says she can "help you to focus it, shape it, and deliver it with passion, excitement and clarity, whether to a reporter, in front of a camera, or to a live audience of thousands." Her list of clients is fun to look at, and pretty impressive.

Index

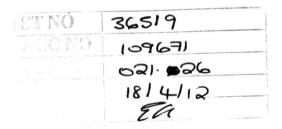

About the Author

In her thirty-something career as a public librarian, Chapple Langemack has done everything from nursing home visits to preschool storytime, not to mention toilets and windows. Her favorite activity, however, is connecting readers and writers.

Her previous book, *The Booktalker's Bible*, was warmly received as an eminently useful and pragmatic guide for novice and seasoned booktalkers ... not to mention very funny.

She currently drives her programming librarians crazy with helpful suggestions about author visits as Senior Managing Librarian at the Bellevue Regional Library for the King County Library System near Seattle. Previously she served as the Readers' Services Coordinator for King County Library System in which role she hosted authors throughout the library system's forty-three branches.

Photograph by Nancy Clendaniel

In demand as a booktalker and a speaker on readers' advisory topics, she has spoken to readers, writers, teachers, and librarians at the local, state, and national levels including the American Library Association (ALA), the Public Library Association, and the National Council of Teachers of English. She has also taught at the University of Washington School of Library and Information Science.

Not content with trying to read herself blind as a member of the ALA's Best Books for Young Adults committee, she went on to serve on the organization's Notable Books Council, a group charged with choosing the year's top twenty-five books for adults. Her optometrist has officially disowned her.

In her non-library time, Chapple is a theatre devotee whose most memorable role involved removing and donning pantyhose on stage. She lives with the world's most amiable husband and two somewhat less amiable cats on Bainbridge Island in Washington State.